Operations Methods

Operations Methods

Waiting Line Applications

Kenneth A. Shaw, PhD

Operations Methods: Waiting Line Applications
Copyright © Business Expert Press, LLC, 2012.

First published in 2011 by
Business Expert Press, LLC
222 East 46th Street, New York, NY 10017
www.businessexpertpress.com

ISBN-13: 978-1-60649-237-6 (paperback)
ISBN-13: 978-1-60649-238-3 (e-book)

DOI 10.4128/9781606492383

A publication in the Business Expert Press Quantitative Approaches to Decision Making collection

Collection ISSN: 2163-9515 (print)
Collection ISSN: 2163-9582 (electronic)

Cover design by Jonathan Pennell
Interior design by Scribe Inc.

First edition: December 2011

10 9 8 7 6 5 4 3 2 1

Printed in the United States of America.

Abstract

The intent of this monograph is to help business practitioners expand their knowledge of waiting line (queuing) analysis and how it can be used to make decisions and improve both service and manufacturing business situations. Readers are assumed to have some familiarity with using probability distributions and Excel analysis tools. Those wishing to refresh their knowledge are provided some brief reviews and references for doing so.

Emphasis is given to discussing the caveats in applying waiting line theory and becoming aware of the assumptions used in developing that theory. The importance of accounting for variability in waiting line processes is discussed in some detail because the basic queuing equations provide only average performance data under steady-state conditions. Understanding how much variability can exist for a given waiting line scenario provides a manager with the insight required to reduce these effects and develop innovative solutions for improving service while reducing operating costs.

In general the mathematical tone of the book is focused on application, not the derivation of the formulas presented. The few derivation exceptions are done to illustrate some approaches not commonly discussed in textbooks—for example, the use of state diagrams and random number approximations of the probability distributions for use in simple simulation models.

To aid in understanding the material presented, some practical examples are given at appropriate points in the text and a few simulation approaches using common spreadsheet software are described.

Keywords

Waiting lines, queues, queuing theory, service rate, arrival rate, utilization, waiting time, multiple servers, service distributions, arrival distributions, cost trade-offs, limited population service, line capacity restrictions, assembly line performance, service process design, service process improvement, simulation methods, Excel applications, Little's Law, variances, stochastic process, state diagrams, priority queues, service classes, deterministic process, memoryless, Markovian, Poisson distribution, exponential distribution, normal distribution, uniform distribution, Erlang distributions, Kendall notation, triangular distribution

Contents

List of Examples ix

Preface xi

Introduction 1

Chapter 1   Concepts, Probabilities, Models, and Costs 5

Chapter 2   The Basics—Single-Channel, Single-Phase Model 17

Chapter 3   The Basics—Multiple-Channel, Single-Phase
             Model 25

Chapter 4   More Complex Single-Channel Models 37

Chapter 5   More Complex Multiple-Channel Models 57

Chapter 6   Managerial Considerations 71

Chapter 7   Useful Tools and Simulation Methods 103

Appendix A Glossary 127

Appendix B Symbol Definitions 135

Appendix C Multiple-Channel Application Data 139

Appendix D Simulation Information 149

Notes 155

References 159

Index 163

Examples

No.	Model	Chapter	Description
2.1	M/M/1	2	Coffee Shop With One Server
3.1	M/M/2	3	Coffee Shop With Two Servers
4.1	M/G/1	4	Coffee Shop Using Various Service Distributions
4.2	M/M/1/K	4	Coffee Shop With Limited Capacity
4.3	M/M/1/∞/N	4	Repair Service With One Server
5.1	M/M/s/∞/N	5	Repair Service With Multiple Servers
5.2	Learning Curve	5	Service Time Reduction Learning Rates
6.1	M/M/1	6	Sandwich Stand Cost Trade-Offs
6.2	M/M/s/∞/N	6	Helicopter Shuttle Business Costs
6.3	M/M/1	6	Factory Inventory Costs
6.4	M/M/1/K	6	Ice Cream Shop With Limited Customer Space
6.5	D/M/1	6	Appointment Schedule Analysis
7.1	M/M/1	7	Data Collection for an M/M/1 Model
7.2	M/M/1	7	Continuous Distribution Determination
7.3	M/M/1	7	Discrete Distribution Determination

Preface

The impetus for writing this book is the product of several conversations with friends and colleagues, an accumulation of professional experiences, and most recently, my interactions with business students and faculty regarding operations and process management improvements.

Nearly a decade ago, I retired from a long career that included individual and managerial responsibilities for a variety of engineering and business functions in several industries; many of these organizations were key players in the development of integrated circuit technology and computer applications. After a year or so working on restoring old cars, taking welding classes, and puttering around a small ranch property, the glow of retirement began to dim. When a former colleague approached me with the proposal of temporarily teaching an operations management course at the local university, I thought it would be an interesting challenge and agreed to do it. Little did I imagine then that this decision would lead to the past 8 years of teaching, new professional relationships, developing new courses, and reviewing several textbooks for authors and publishers.

The increased focus on supply chain principles and their business considerations in a global economy has often resulted in less classroom time in many business school curriculums for more in-depth coverage of specific operations methods, such as queuing analysis, linear programming, simulation methods, and the factors affecting the variability of the predicted results of such methods. As a result, these topics are often provided as chapter supplements on DVDs or the Internet for recent editions of operations management textbooks, and many methods are only briefly discussed in undergraduate classes. The expectation is that if students are made aware of the existence of these methods and if their use is needed in a future career, our graduates will be able to educate themselves regarding that use.

Discussions regarding this situation with my academic colleagues and some of the authors whose books I have reviewed indicate a need for small books focused on different operations methods to help senior-level students and business graduates in that self-education. This monograph on waiting lines will hopefully satisfy part of that need.

It is important that I acknowledge the valued discussions, advice, and inputs provided by several of my colleagues and friends and the professionals at Business Expert Press and Scribe. These individuals include the following:

- John Sloan, Zhaohui Wu, Rene Reitsma, V. T. Raja, Michael Curry, James Moran, Bryon Marshall, and Erik Larson in the College of Business at Oregon State University.
- James and Mona Fitzsimmons, who coauthored the textbook[1] used in one of my courses and whose work provided me with a number of good ideas. They were the ones who inspired me to begin this book.
- David Parker, Scott Eisenberg, and Cindy Durand of Business Expert Press who provided encouragement, great feedback, and patience during the completion of the text.
- Rachel Paul McGrath and her editing colleagues at Scribe.

Last, but far from least, I must express my thanks and appreciation to my wife, Judy, and our children, Rachel and Jeremy, for their patience and encouragement as I strived to understand business processes better over the years.

Introduction

When waiting line (queuing) theory is introduced in business or engineering classes, students are presented fundamental rules and equations that give consistent results for the same set of conditions. This simplifies the initial discussion of often complex issues to enable students to become comfortable with the basic concepts and obtain the average results for various waiting line performance measures. Later, usually at the graduate level, the pesky details regarding the real-life variability in these average values are revealed to explain why the predictions provided by the fundamental rules rarely are exactly true. As many of you no doubt recognize, this last statement also applies to many other disciplines and thus should be considered a basic fact of life.

The tone and scope of this monograph assumes that you, the reader, are a person who has already taken the initiative to increase your understanding of the waiting line and associated service aspects of your business, with the goal of either improving service, reducing operating cost, or both. You have probably reviewed your old college texts, talked to some more experienced colleagues, reviewed the literature available in the local library, and used Internet search engines to find sites that might help. A common result is that you probably noticed that many of the equations provided by different authors do not appear to be the same for a particular performance measure, such as average waiting time or line length. Another outcome is that you often encounter different terms used for what appears to be the same concept. My goal is help you navigate through these apparent discrepancies, introduce you to some new concepts that are likely to be unfamiliar, and help you achieve a better understanding for your business needs. So let us begin.

We begin by reviewing the fundamental rules for different waiting line models and then expand the discussion to cover some of those all-too-frequent occasions where what we observe in actual practice does not seem to agree with the predicted values. These variations should not be viewed with dismay, however, but rather as opportunities for innovating, developing a competitive advantage, and assessing possible business risks.

Some mention of the level of mathematic understanding expected of you is appropriate at this point. Several of the performance expressions will intuitively make sense. Others will require you to accept their validity on faith because the mathematics behind their derivation can be quite daunting to someone who is not a mathematician. For the most part, we will not discuss the derivation of most formulas because this monograph is focused on application. However, we will occasionally need to delve more deeply into how a few formulas are derived so we can understand their limitations in predicting actual business outcomes. In addition, we will develop some expressions that, while not exactly mathematically rigorous, will provide good enough approximations for pragmatic business decisions.

The following is likely to be the most useful and important piece of advice you can gain from reading this monograph: As people gain experience in business, they develop a gut feeling as to what the ballpark estimate of the results of a business analysis will be. Hence when the calculated result does not agree with their estimate, they double-check the calculations. Because of the probabilistic content in waiting line equations, it is more difficult to acquire an intuitive feeling as to what the result should be. Many of the waiting line equations can be quite complex, and the likelihood of typographical errors in equations presented in references and other material is increased. In fact, I discovered formula errors and other formula differences in many of the references consulted during my research for this monograph. Some of these are obvious to an astute reader, but others can take considerable effort to detect.

Therefore, I cannot stress enough how important it is to make sure that the units of measure for each parameter in a waiting line equation are accounted for and that their use balances out into the proper units for the answer. Consistent checking of the units in your answers will help indicate the presence of errors, whether they are caused by an error in the equation, an incorrect entry in the equation, or a calculation error on your part.

Chapter 1 reviews the basic concepts used for waiting line process analysis; discusses the most common probability distributions; and introduces state diagrams that are used to derive many queuing formulas, descriptions and notation for different waiting line models, and basic cost considerations.

Chapter 2 covers the characteristics and analysis of basic single-channel, single-phase models common to small businesses and sections of manufacturing lines. Chapter 3 covers the characteristics and analysis of basic multiple-channel, single-phase models like most of us have encountered in banks and post offices. You can skip these chapters if you feel that you are sufficiently familiar with the basics; but there are some useful clarifications not usually discussed in college textbooks that will be helpful when we address more complex situations.

Chapters 4 and 5 cover more complex concepts related to less common arrival and service distributions, line capacity limitations, limited population applications commonly used for maintenance activities, multiple-server situations, and manufacturing applications. Chapter 5 also includes equations for direct computations of limited population models to allow you to use spreadsheet methods instead of finite queuing tables. Some new nomenclature is introduced to help avoid some confusion that can occur when using such equations.

Chapter 6 focuses on managerial considerations regarding waiting line decisions. The limitation that commonly used waiting line equations predict only average performance is discussed in some detail. Knowing more about performance variability is necessary to enable managerial consideration to reduce its effects on customer service and operating costs. Some possible strategies and methods for reducing variability in both the arrival and the service rates are reviewed, and some cost decisions, such as cost trade-offs between adding service capacity versus process improvements, are discussed. Chapter 6 also discusses some of the softer factors, such as waiting line psychology, priority management, and preferred customer treatment.

In Chapter 7, several tools are discussed. The first is Little's Law, a useful mathematical expression relating waiting line length to waiting time using the arrival rate. The use of Little's Law as a handy method to obtain some useful starting data about a waiting line situation without requiring extensive data gathering over extended periods of time is also described. To gain knowledge about performance variability for the evaluation of best- and worst-case scenarios, simulation is required. Some examples show how simulation models can be constructed for several waiting line situations using functions commonly available in Excel 2007 or 2010.

A list of references is provided at the end. Appendix A provides a glossary of terms; appendix B lists symbols used with their definitions; appendix C presents some useful tables and spreadsheet examples for multiple-server applications; and appendix D provides some useful simulation design information for Excel users.

CHAPTER 1

Concepts, Probabilities, Models, and Costs

Standing in line for some service is a universal human experience. We all have had the experience of choosing one line that appears to be moving the fastest only to observe later that an adjacent line is now moving faster. The reality is that all customers do not have the same service requirements, and even if they do, that service does not always take the same amount of time to complete.

Some of us are prepared to ask for what we need when we reach the server; others are still making up their minds as to exactly what they want. The process of paying for the service also adds to service time variability. How many of us have watched the person being served in front of us take a considerable amount of time collecting belongings and finding money or a credit card to pay the server while another customer is more organized, has exact change, and moves out of the line quickly when the service is completed. Such observations are important because they illustrate that one way to improve customer service is to help customers be better prepared when they reach the server. An illustration of this in practice is the security line process at many airports.

An important consideration for service businesses is being able to estimate how many customers might arrive during a given time period T. It is also important to know the nature of customer arrivals. Are they at regular intervals, random, one at a time, in groups, or in some other way? Given this information and the internal knowledge of how long service usually takes, businesses can use waiting line analysis to determine how many servers are needed to provide an acceptable level of performance at a reasonable cost. Some other performance measures of possible interest are as follows:

- How long is the average line?
- What is the typical waiting time before being served?
- What is the probability that the line will exceed the available waiting space?
- If one server is not enough to satisfy demand, how many more servers are needed?
- What is the probability that a customer will not have to wait in line?
- How much do we have to reduce average service time to avoid adding another server?
- Which is more cost-effective—buying a new automated machine to handle part of the demand or hiring more servers?
- What effect would setting up separate lines for different classes of customers have on overall service performance and operating costs?

When applying queuing theory to factory applications, some waiting line parameters are more easily controlled; others become more complex, particularly when more than one process step (phase) is involved. Production scheduling more easily controls variability in the arrival rate. The service rate variability is usually constrained when manufacturing items but can vary the same as when dealing with customers if the factory is providing repairs or custom items with varying work flows. Moving items between batch and one-at-a-time processes are also analytical challenges. Performance measures of possible interest in such applications include the following:

- What is the average throughput?
- What is the typical processing time?
- What is the line capacity and which step limits it?
- What is the average amount of work in process (WIP)?
- How much capacity is needed for the inventory (queue) before each step?
- How do you handle mixed job flows?

In some cases, basic queuing equations can be used to provide rough approximations to some of these manufacturing questions. For more accurate estimates, however, simulation methods are required. For those who do not want to develop their own applications, a variety of vendors have produced simulation programs for common situations. However, it is important if you take either path toward using simulation that you are aware of the assumptions and queuing models available. Selecting the wrong model for your application will not provide useful results no matter how sophisticated the simulation package is.

Managerial considerations regarding the previous performance questions and others are discussed in chapter 6. Many of them have different options depending on the waiting line model(s) used. Chapter 7 discusses some simple simulation applications and how a simple model can be used as a building block for more complex simulations. Appendix D provides information for using Excel for some basic simulations. Appendix B defines the symbols used throughout this monograph. Because three of these symbols are necessary to any discussion of waiting line situations, analysis, models, or concepts, they need to be defined here:

λ: the *average* arrival rate of customers or items seeking service

μ: the *average* service rate

ρ: the ratio λ/μ, often referred to as the utilization factor

The fundamental assumption of waiting line analysis is that the behavior of customer arrivals and service times can be described by appropriate probability distributions given the average interarrival time $1/\lambda$, the average service time $1/\mu$, and some knowledge of the pool of possible customers (the "calling population") to be served.[1] Many of the waiting line performance measure formulas discussed in this chapter are a result of this assumption combined with the insight and the contributions of many talented individuals and organizations.

We will accept most of these formulas without derivation except when a partial or a complete derivation is necessary to gain a better understanding of what a particular formula does or does not address. For those interested in such derivations and some good application examples, the books by Laguna and Marklund[2] on business process modeling and Hillier and Lieberman[3] on operations research are useful references. Another reference is Nelson's book[4] on modeling stochastic processes.

The most commonly used probability distributions are the Poisson distribution for discrete values and the exponential distribution for continuous values with the assumption that the calling population is infinite. Other distributions are used when some control over the arrival rate or the service time is possible and when the population pool or the waiting line capacity is limited.

In selecting distributions, it is important to select an appropriate time interval for data collection and the analysis on which the average values for arrival and service rates can be based. The average waiting line performance measures are independent of the time interval chosen, which will be shown later when using the formulas. You will lose sight of how much the arrival rate can vary during the day if you choose an interval that is too large.

Poisson Distribution

The Poisson distribution is a discrete distribution because there are no fractional arrivals. It is described by Equation 1.1, where P(n) is the probability that n arrivals will arrive during time interval T given an average arrival rate of λ:

$$P(n) = \frac{(\lambda T)^n e^{-\lambda T}}{n!} \quad \text{for } n = 0, 1, 2, \dots \qquad (1.1)$$

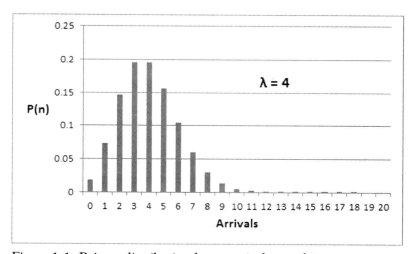

Figure 1.1. Poisson distribution for an arrival rate of 4.

The Poisson distribution for an average arrival rate of 4 is shown in Figure 1.1. It is important to note that there is a finite probability that no arrivals will occur during the time interval on which the average rate is based. Knowing this value—often designated as P_0 rather than $P(0)$—is very useful in business decisions, as we will discuss in chapter 6.

Another useful property is that adding individual Poisson distributions results in another Poisson distribution. Conversely, breaking down a Poisson distribution into two or more separate distributions results in a set of two or more Poisson distributions. This is advantageous when adding together the known arrival rates of individual classes of customers or determining the effect of diverting a part of an existing arrival distribution to a new branch office. We will discuss this in more detail in chapter 6.

Exponential Distribution

An exponential distribution is a versatile probability distribution that is used to describe both service times and the times between arrivals in waiting line scenarios. It is most often expressed by Equation 1.2, where $P(time > t)$ is the probability that the service time or the interarrival time will be greater than time t, setting $\alpha = \mu$ for service time probabilities and $\alpha = \lambda$ for interarrival time probabilities:

$$P(time > t) = e^{-\alpha t} \text{ for } t \geq 0. \tag{1.2}$$

The exponential distributions for two average service rates of 3 and 6.5 are shown in Figure 1.2. Your intuition that the probability of a task requiring a given completion time should decrease as the service rate increases is now validated. You should also note that a probability of 36.79%[5] corresponds to the average service time of $1/\mu$.

An exponential probability distribution has the property of being "memoryless." That is, its predictions of what happens next are independent of what has happened before. For example, the probability at any given moment that the next customer will arrive in 2 minutes is the same whether the previous customer arrived a few seconds ago or an hour ago. Such a distribution is also referred to as being "Markovian" and is indicated by the symbol M in the waiting line model notation described later in this chapter. More common examples of this property are the probability of the next coin flip being heads or the next roll of two dice adding up

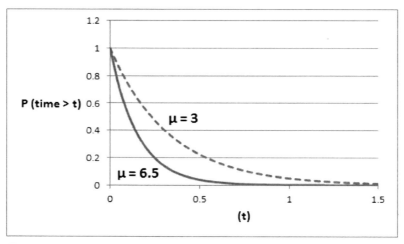

Figure 1.2. Exponential distributions for service rates of 3 and 6.5.

to five. The odds of either occurring are unaffected by any knowledge of the results of previous coin flips or dice throws.

Other Probability Distributions

In many service scenarios, the performance data collected will indicate that either the arrival or the service characteristics are not well represented by Poisson and exponential distributions. For example, consider a coffee shop where there is a mix of customers, some who just want a standard cup of coffee and others who want more customized lattes and mochas. In addition, while the exponential distribution allows the probability of very short service times, in practice, the minimum time required to serve a customer is greater than those values. If we want to evaluate more than the average performance values, this mix of relatively constant and varying service times plus a minimum time limit usually does not fit well with using a single exponential distribution.

Also, consider standardized service situations where the service times are more predictable (deterministic). In such cases, normal distributions or even constant values can be used. This situation is discussed in more detail in chapter 4.

A variant of the Erlang[6] distribution can be used to determine the number of customers turned away by insufficient capacity, and phase-type distributions can be used to characterize waiting lines with more than one phase in sequence. When there is more than one phase in a channel, the mathematics for analytical expressions describing waiting line performance becomes much more challenging. In such cases, we can make some approximations or use computer simulation to provide more useful insight for business applications. One example is a production line with several assembly operations. This situation is discussed in more detail in chapters 4 and 7.

State Diagrams and Balance Equations

The intent of this monograph is not to make you an expert on deriving waiting line expressions; however, it is useful to spend some time discussing how state diagrams are used to develop some of the simpler formulas. This then provides a better understanding of the relationships between arrival rates, service rates, and the probabilities of different line conditions, such as nobody in line (P_0), two people in line (P_2), and so forth.

Figure 1.3 shows a generic state diagram where each hexagon represents a specific number of customers in a single-channel waiting line. In this case, we will keep it simple by limiting the maximum number of customers in the system to two. This is not a far-fetched simplification because it could represent an independent stockbroker's telephone with a capacity for only one call on hold.

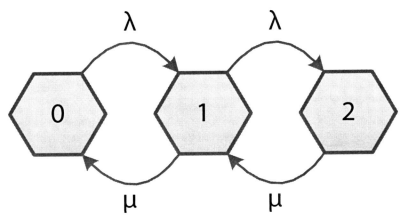

Figure 1.3. State diagram for a single-channel waiting line.

To obtain an intuitive feel for what this diagram represents, we first consider the first two states on the left (state 2 is ignored for now). One can see that the *maximum* flow from the state of no customers in the system to the state of one customer in the system is the arrival rate λ. The *maximum* flow back to a state of no customers is the service rate μ. If both the arrival and the service rates are constant with no variability, then the proportion of time each state exists is determined by the difference between the arrival and the service rates. This then requires the service rate to be greater than the arrival rate to avoid the need for further states to account for inadequate capacity.

So, what is missing in this state diagram? While it may be obvious to the frequent state diagram user, it often is not obvious to many business students. The key factor here and the magic behind using state diagrams to develop queuing analysis formulas is that each state has a probability of existence that allows the rates into a state to equal the rates from that state. Such balance equations allow one to determine the probability for each state in terms of the given average arrival and service rates. This becomes particularly important when the distributions for the arrival and the service rates are taken into account. Then an overflow to higher states is necessary for situations when a momentary burst of customers overwhelms the service rate and results in more customers in the system.

For example, the balance equations (inputs equal outputs) for the three states in Figure 1.3 are as follows:

$$\text{State 0: } (P_1 \times \mu) = (P_0 \times \lambda),$$
$$\text{State 1: } (P_0 \times \lambda) + (P_2 \times \mu) = (P_1 \times \lambda) + (P_1 \times \mu), \qquad (1.3)$$
$$\text{State 2: } (P_1 \times \lambda) = (P_2 \times \mu).$$

Given the set of balance equations for all the possible states, the individual probabilities for steady-state behavior can be derived. For example, we first use the equation for State 0 to solve for P_0 in terms of P_1. Then, using the requirement that the sum of all probabilities must be equal to 1, we solve for P_2 in terms of P_1 and P_0. That is, $P_2 = 1 - P_1 - P_0 = 1 - P_1 - [(\mu/\lambda) \times P_1]$. Substituting these results for P_0 and P_2 in the equation for State 1, we can then determine the value for P_1 in terms of ρ. Knowing P_1, we can then obtain the values for P_0 and P_2 using the equations for States 0 and 2. The following results are produced:

$$P_0 = 1/(1 + \rho + \rho^2),$$
$$P_1 = \rho/(1 + \rho + \rho^2), \qquad (1.4)$$
$$P_2 = \rho^2/(1 + \rho + \rho^2).$$

If our calculations are correct, the sum of P_0, P_1, and P_2 should equal 1, which they do. What is also useful here is having answers requiring only the utilization factor ρ. This may not always be the case, but it simplifies the analysis when it is.

For a larger number of states, the mathematics involved can be quite daunting. However, for a queuing situation, where the number of states is limited by physical constraints such as a finite calling population, limited line length, or the number of phone lines, state diagrams can be quite useful in obtaining useful expressions without having to employ extensive mathematical methods. We will return to this state diagram when we discuss the more complex aspects of single-channel waiting lines in chapter 4.

Waiting Line Models and Notation

Although there is some commonality across various waiting line models, such as Little's Law which is discussed in chapter 7, many of the formulas predicting various performance measures are dependent on the type of model used. Most references use Kendall's notation[7] to identify which waiting line situation they are discussing. The original notation reportedly had just three characteristics, A/B/C, indicating, in order, the nature of the arrival distribution, the service distribution, and the number of channels or servers. This notation has been expanded over time to five or six characteristics, A/B/C/d/e/f, to include values for the limit on line length, the size of the calling population, and the priority rule used to process customers.

You will find in various references that there is no consistent order for indicating the last three characteristics or even for using all three. Hence, it is important to note that here we will use the d/e/f sequence defined in the previous paragraph. The symbols used to designate the various probability distributions are defined in appendix B. For example, the single-channel, single-phase model discussed in chapter 2 is given the notation M/M/1/∞/∞/FCFS, where M indicates the choice of Markovian distributions for the arrival and the service rates. In most references, this notation is shortened to M/M/1.

Priority Rules

Unless specified otherwise, a first-come, first served (FCFS) priority rule is assumed for most waiting line situations. This rule can also be expressed as a first-in, first-out (FIFO) priority. Customers consider this to be the fairest approach, particularly when other customers waiting in line are visible.

However, there are situations where an FCFS rule is not the best approach, such as the processing of patients in a hospital emergency room. Obviously, there will be some patients with more urgent needs for care than others, regardless of their place in the arrival sequence. Another example is travelers waiting in line to check in at the airport. When the lines at airline ticket counters become long at peak periods and the waiting time becomes greater than the time to flight departure for some travelers, some process is required to expedite the ticket and baggage check-in processing for those passengers.

Not so obvious is the desire by many service operations to give some preference to their more important customers. When customers can see other customers waiting, this desire can be satisfied by having dedicated servers for the more important customers. Examples are the frequent flyer lines at the airport, a business-only teller window at the bank, or a window dedicated for package pickup at the post office.

More solutions for providing preferential treatment to selected customers are available when customers cannot view other customers waiting. One example is a call center for a financial institution. Such solutions are discussed in more detail in chapter 5.

In a manufacturing line situation, you may want a system for expediting critical orders, often referred to as "hot lots," while also taking care to avoid any given item from being delayed too long because of preemptions by expedited orders. This is especially important if the customer-ordering process frequently accepts too many rush orders. Part of the solution is managerial policy, which is discussed in chapter 6. In addition, you can take advantage of computer methods for managing the sequence of items being processed, which is described in chapter 7.

Finally, although rarely discussed in most waiting line textbooks, effective methods are needed to deal with rude, unruly, or disruptive customers. Considering how your business addresses such incidents before they actually occur is especially important when such behavior is visible to other customers.

Cost Curves

The relationship between operation costs and the costs of waiting is illustrated in many references by similar versions of the simplified graph shown in Figure 1.4. As more servers are hired, customers have to wait less, but the costs of doing business increase. This trade-off between customer service and operating costs is shown in Figure 1.4 to have a minimum value that intuitively would appear to be the desired business solution.

However, this simplified model does not depict actual conditions for many service businesses, particularly since the operations costs rarely increase in a linear fashion. So, you may ask, how does one obtain the actual waiting costs for a particular situation? The costs related to adding more servers or items being out of service while they wait for maintenance are more easily determined than the costs of unhappy customers. Some marketing firms have done surveys about how much a typical customer

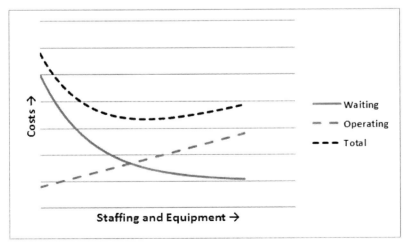

Figure 1.4. Waiting line cost relationships.

is willing to wait for service or what length of line will discourage a customer from even entering it. But you need to be wary of this information unless such surveys have been done for your particular type of service in your locality. Even then, you should recognize that customer attitudes will vary from one day to the next, depending on whether or not customers are in a good mood, are in a hurry, or are with friends in line; the weather is sunny or miserable; and so forth. Did the marketing group survey people actually in line under different conditions or did they just interview a group of people about their service preferences?

Is your service one of choice—like buying a cup of coffee—or one of necessity—like obtaining a new driver's license? Do you have several competitors or are you the only choice for the service? In the latter situations, customers may not like the performance provided but must put up with it because there are no other alternatives available. This is often the case with government agencies, where the trade-off is better service or lower taxes.

In addition, operating costs are rarely linear, as implied in Figure 1.4. Increases in equipment and the number of servers create jumps in operating costs. Facility additions and other fixed costs required to support additional servers and equipment must be accounted for, and the effect on other behind-the-scenes (back office) support costs should be considered.

Waiting line costs are also not always linear. Waiting a few minutes longer may be inconvenient, but waiting long enough for a meal to get cold or to miss a deadline like a scheduled transportation departure can cause the cost to increase significantly.

These costs and some suggested methods for managing them are discussed in more detail in chapter 6.

CHAPTER 2

The Basics—
Single-Channel,
Single-Phase Model

A single line of people waiting for some service is arguably the most common business model on our planet (see Figure 2.1 for a diagram of this configuration). The variations on this simple theme are nearly infinite when you consider the forms that the service can take and the nature of the customers desiring that service.

We will use a coffee shop where customers from different walks of life enter the shop; wait in line; and, when they reach the service window, order anything from a simple cup of coffee to a more complex mixture of coffee and other ingredients to larger orders of multiple combinations of these. To analyze the basic behavior of this model, we must make some assumptions where the full Kendall notation for the model is M/M/1/∞/∞/FCFS:

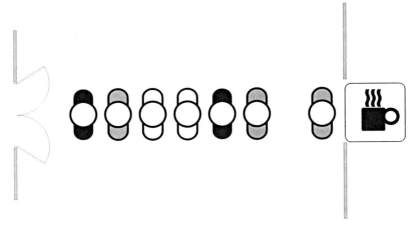

Figure 2.1. M/M/1 configuration.

- The arrival rate distribution is described by a Poisson distribution using an average rate λ, which means that the interarrival times can be characterized by an exponential distribution with an average interarrival time of $1/\lambda$. Interarrival times are independent of the number of customers in the system.
- The service time distribution is defined by an exponential distribution with an average service time of $1/\mu$, where μ represents the average service rate. Service times are independent of the number of customers in the system.
- The number of channels (servers) is one, and the number of phases in the service is one. We assume here that a single server does everything for the customer in the coffee shop: taking the order, preparing the coffee, and collecting the payment. Obviously, in many coffee shops with a higher volume of customers, more than one person likely performs these activities. We will discuss these complexities in chapter 4.
- The arrival or calling population is infinite in size. This avoids complications introduced by the possibility of having served all available customers.
- The length of the waiting line can be infinite. Although not really possible in real-world situations, this avoids analysis complications introduced by the rare possibility that some customers are blocked from entering the line. We will discuss the effects of limited line lengths in later chapters.
- The priority rule is first come, first served (FCFS).
- Balking or reneging by customers is not considered in the analysis.
- The average arrival rate is less than the average service rate ($\lambda < \mu$). That is, the utilization factor $\rho = \lambda/\mu$ is less than 1.

This last assumption should be intuitively obvious because the average line length will increase significantly when the arrival rate approaches the service rate, as shown in Figure 2.2.

One thing that is often confusing when reviewing the equations presented by different authors for a given waiting line model is that at first glance they do not always appear to be the same. However, with closer inspection, we can see that one version is equivalent to another version

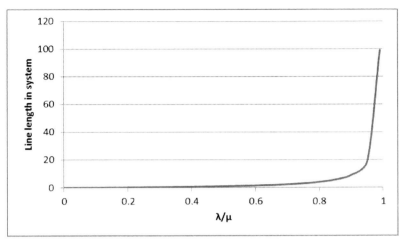

Figure 2.2. Increase in average line length as $\lambda \to \mu$.

because some author(s) substituted ρ for some combinations of λ and μ or have applied Little's Law. The different versions are provided here for your reference with what I consider to be the most useful version listed first. The various performance measures for the basic M/M/1 model are listed in the same order in which they will be presented for other waiting line models later in the book.

- Utilization factor: $\rho = \lambda/\mu$; for a basic M/M/1 model, ρ must be less than 1.
- Probability of 0 customers in the system (this is also the probability that a customer will experience no waiting for service): $P_0 = 1 - \rho$.
- Probability of exactly n customers in the system: $P_n = (1 - \rho)\rho^n = P_0\rho^n$.
- Probability that the number of customers in the system is greater than k:

$$P_{n>k} = \rho^{k+1}.$$

- Probability that the server is busy: $P_{n>0} = 1 - P_0 = \rho$.
- Average number of customers in the system:

$$L = \lambda/(\mu - \lambda) = \rho/(1 - \rho) = \lambda W.$$

- Average total time customers spend in the system: $W = 1/(\mu - \lambda) = L/\lambda$.
- Average number of customers waiting in the queue (not yet being served):

$$L_q = \rho L = \rho\lambda/(\mu - \lambda) = \lambda^2/[\mu(\mu - \lambda)] = \rho^2/(1 - \rho) = L - \rho = \lambda W_q.$$

- Average time customers wait in the queue before being served:

$$W_q = \rho W = W - (1/\mu) = \rho/(\mu - \lambda) = \lambda/[\mu(\mu - \lambda)] = L_q/\lambda.$$

The term *system* applies to not only the number of customers waiting in line but also any customer(s) being served. Also useful to remember is that the sum of all possible probabilities for a parameter must equal 1. This allows you to determine a probability that may be difficult to calculate directly. In such a case, you add together all the other possible probabilities excluding the one you want to determine and subtract that sum from 1. An example of this was shown previously for the probability that a server is busy.

If you observe the formulas for line lengths and waiting time carefully, you can see that the ratio of the average number of people in the system to the average waiting time in that system is equal to the average arrival rate when the system is in a steady-state condition. Expressed in the form $L = \lambda W$, this ratio is referred to as Little's Law.[1] This ratio also applies when just considering the number of people waiting in line and the time spent waiting in that line before being served. As we will see in subsequent chapters, Little's Law applies across a wide range of waiting line models regardless of the probability distributions chosen to represent the arrival and the service rates. Hence, Little's Law is especially useful for manufacturing applications of queuing analysis where such probability distributions are often unknown.

Another significant observation can be drawn by looking at the formulas for L, L_q, and P_0 that are expressed using only the utilization factor $\rho = \lambda/\mu$. This means that these values vary only with ρ; that is, as long as the arrival and service rates increase in direct proportion to each other (ρ remains constant), the values for L, L_q, and P_0 will remain unchanged. However, W and W_q will decrease with increasing values of λ and μ. Figure 2.2 shows the value for L versus ρ, and you can see that the line length is essentially flat for $\rho < 0.4$. In chapter 3, you will see that this characteristic holds true for multiple-channel lines.

You may observe what appears to be an inconsistency in the expressions for L_q, where it is shown as being equal to both ρL and $L - \rho$. Is this possible? Most textbooks avoid this question by presenting only one version for L_q; however, I include both versions in my class lectures as a check on whether students are reading the material. To answer the question: If both equations are true, then ρL must equal $L - \rho$. Moving all the L terms to one side of the equation gives the result that $L(1 - \rho) = \rho$. Dividing both sides by $(1 - \rho)$ gives $L = \rho/(1 - \rho)$, which is the equation for L.

Example 2.1. Coffee Shop With One Server

To gain a more comfortable understanding of how the preceding performance measures can be used, consider a small coffee shop we will call Ken's Caffeine Fix. The shop is located in a downtown area and provides various forms of coffee to nearby office workers who stop in for a cup of their favorite brew at various times of the day. We will make two assumptions: (1) The average arrival rate does not vary during the day, and (2) the owner performs all parts of the service provided: takes the order, prepares the coffee, and collects the payment. The issues created by arrival rates varying during the day and having a helper do parts of the service will be discussed in later chapters. To assign some values to this operation, let us assume that it takes an average of 2 minutes to serve each customer, and the average number of customers per hour is 24.

This gives us an average arrival rate λ of 24 customers per hour and an average service rate μ of 1 customer per 2 minutes = 30 customers/hour. This illustrates a critical consideration when analyzing waiting line situations—the arrival rate must be less than the service rate.

Many businesses collect operating data in this way: the average number of customers per some time period and the typical service time. Thus some conversion of the data is necessary because the time references for the arrival and service rates must be the same. A real-life example of collecting data for coffee shops on a college campus will be given in chapter 7.

The utilization factor ρ is 24/30 = 0.8 or 80%. This is the probability that the owner will be busy serving a customer when the next customer enters the shop. Hence the probability of no customers in the shop (P_0) is $1 - \rho = 20\%$. This is a useful value to know because the owner needs some time during each hour to replenish the cream-and-sugar station, brew more regular coffee, and do general cleanup.

The average number of customers in the shop (L) is expected to be $24/(30 - 24) = 4$ customers, and the average number waiting in line (L_q) is $0.8 \times 4 = 3.2$ customers. You should recognize that these values are independent of the time period chosen. If the owner had collected data on customer arrivals and service times over a sequence of 15-minute periods rather than hours, the results for L and L_q would be the same. In other words, because the utilization factor is unchanged, L and L_q are unchanged. That is, the average line length is independent of the time reference for the average arrival and service rates.

The average total time spent by customers getting their coffee is $60/(30 - 24) = 10$ minutes, and the time spent waiting in line is $0.8 \times 10 = 8$ minutes. This obviously is too long for an office worker just wanting a quick cup of regular coffee. Ways to shorten the wait for this class of customer are discussed in chapter 6. Of interest here is that Little's Law indicates the waiting time decreases as the arrival rate increases, *provided* that the utilization factor remains constant (the service rate increases proportionately with the arrival rate).

Figure 2.3 shows typical individual waiting times and service (brewing) times along with the number of customers already in the shop when each customer arrives. These values were obtained using a simple Excel simulation program. This set of sample data does not show any values for L that are greater than 5, which could lead a person to assume that the line lengths for the business are not too long. However, subsequent simulation runs using the same interarrival and service time distributions and the same number of customers have demonstrated possible line lengths as great as 14, brewing times as long as 16 minutes, and waiting times up to 20 minutes. To obtain more information regarding the variability of the performance measures, multiple simulation runs are required. These will be explored in detail in chapter 7. You should note in Figure 2.3 that the average for each

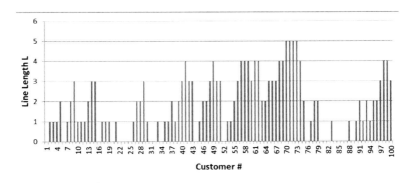

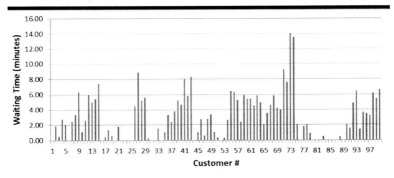

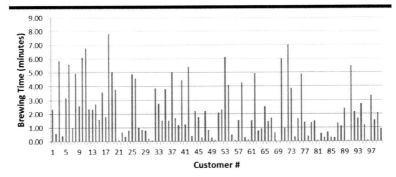

Figure 2.3. Some typical performance values for the first 100 customers entering a typical coffee shop.

performance measure depicted rarely occurs, if at all, for any customer. *This leads to a very important observation that the average performance values derived from the queuing equations are primarily for the longer-term business perspective and are a very poor indicator of what a typical customer encounters.*

As mentioned in chapter 1, an exponential distribution is not the most accurate distribution to represent the service time for this type of business because the minimum service time required for even a simple cup of house coffee is likely to be greater than 30 seconds when the time for payment is included. Yet the simulated data in Figure 2.3 show several occasions when the brewing time is less than 30 seconds (0.5 minute). The longer brewing times shown can be expected when one considers a customer ordering several coffees for a group of people. Perhaps an Erlang distribution with an appropriate k factor would be a better representation for this type of service, as discussed in chapter 4.

Finally, market surveys can provide estimates of how long a line can be before customers looking into the shop are likely to decide to not even enter (balking). For example, let us say that a line longer than 5 people, including the person being served, is a definite turnoff for a potential coffee shop customer. So, given the data for this example, what is the probability of this occurring? Referring to the data in Example 2.1 and using the formula $P_{n>k} = \rho^{k+1}$, where k = 5, we obtain $0.8^6 = 0.2621$ or 26.21%.

Thus, Ken's Caffeine Fix coffee shop in Example 2.1 is likely to lose at least one fourth of its possible customers. Conversely, the probability that the average number of customers in the shop is 5 or less is $1 - 0.2621 = 0.7379$ or 73.79%.

CHAPTER 3

The Basics—
Multiple-Channel,
Single-Phase Model

When the demand exceeds the output of a business, either that business must become more productive, increasing its output rate to cope with the increased demand, or adding more capacity to satisfy it. In a service situation, you either reduce your average service time per server or you add more servers. In this chapter, we will expand the waiting line analysis to take into account the effects of adding more servers. In chapter 6, we will explore the alternative of reducing service time.

Figure 3.1 shows a simple multiple-channel, single-phase model M/M/s with two servers. Two queue configurations are possible: a separate line for each server and one queue feeding both servers.

Grocery and retail store checkout lines, traffic lanes, and old-style ticket counters are common examples of the separate lines configuration, and most banks and post offices are common examples of the single line configuration[1] that directs each customer to the next available server. Some authors refer to the single line arrangement as a "snake" configuration because it often requires a winding layout to accommodate its length. A common example is the arrangement at airports before the passenger security checkpoints.

You may think that analyzing this will be easy. All you would have to do is either multiply the service rate by the number of servers for a single line feeding two servers or divide the arrival rate in half for two separate lines and then use the performance measures discussed in chapter 2 for the single-channel, single-phase model M/M/1. However, this is incorrect for a single service location with more than one server because the number of customers for one server *is not independent* of the number of

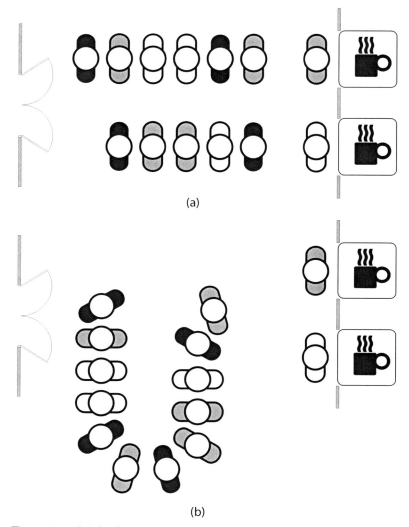

(a)

(b)

Figure 3.1. Multiple-server waiting line configurations: (a) separate line per server and (b) one line feeding both servers.

customers for the other server. There are other nuances to be considered, such as the probability of no customers for one server when the other server is still busy, the probability that a newly arriving customer will pick a particular line in the separate line per server configuration, or the probability that a customer in a slowly moving line will change lines to a more quickly moving line (a process called jockeying).

To analyze the basic behavior of this model, we must make some assumptions, where the full Kendall notation for the model is M/M/s/∞/∞/FCFS:

- The arrival rate distribution is described by a Poisson distribution using an average rate λ, which means that the interarrival times can be characterized by an exponential distribution with an average interarrival time of $1/\lambda$. Interarrival times are independent of the number of customers in the system.
- The service time distribution for each server is defined by an exponential distribution with an average service time of $1/\mu$, where μ represents the average service rate. The service rates are the same[2] for each server. Obviously, a new server is likely to not be as productive as an experienced server. However, keep in mind that the waiting line equations are based on a steady-state condition, which implies that the new server has attained the average service rate capability. How long this may take is discussed in more detail in chapter 5.
- Service times are independent of the number of customers in the system.
- The number of phases in the service is one. We are assuming here that each server can do everything for the customer in the respective business: take the customer's request, perform the necessary actions, and collect any payment. However, in many businesses where there is a higher volume of customers and several employees, some of these actions are likely to be assigned to only one or more of the servers. We will discuss some of these complexities in chapter 5.
- The arrival or calling population is infinite in size. This avoids complications introduced by the possibility of having served all available customers.
- The length of the waiting line(s) can be infinite. Although not really possible in real-world situations, this avoids analysis complications introduced by the rare possibility that some customers are blocked from entering the line. We will discuss the effects of limited line lengths in later chapters.
- The priority rule is first come, first served (FCFS).

- Balking or reneging by customers is not considered in the analysis.
- Jockeying is allowed in separate line configurations.
- The average arrival rate is less than the average total service rate ($\lambda < s\mu$). That is, the multichannel utilization factor ($\rho_s = \lambda/s\mu$) is less than 1.

This last requirement clarifies an error that occasionally occurs: Some texts consistently use a value for ρ as defined for the M/M/1 model in their equations for the M/M/s model, while other texts use a ρ value equivalent to ρ_s but without the s subscript to indicate that their use of ρ has a different definition in the M/M/s equations. In this monograph, ρ always represents λ/μ, and ρ_s is used to represent $\lambda/s\mu$. Thus, $\rho_s = \rho/s$. For a given average arrival rate and an average service rate per server, the minimum number of servers must then be greater than λ/μ. The actual number of servers for many situations is likely to be greater than this minimum number to achieve desired performance values.

As for the M/M/1 model discussed in chapter 2, there are different versions of some of the performance measure equations in the literature regarding queuing analysis. Some alternate versions are provided here for your reference, with what I consider to be the more common version listed first. The various performance measures are listed in the same order as they are presented for the M/M/1 model in chapter 2. Additional measures special to the M/M/s model are discussed in chapter 5. You are reminded that the term *system* includes not only the number of customers waiting in line but also the customer(s) being served.

- M/M/s utilization factor: $\rho_s = \lambda/s\mu$: for an M/M/s model, this value must be less than 1 for the following equations to be valid.
- Probability of zero customers in the system: The equation for P_0 here is more complicated:[3]

$$P_0 = \frac{1}{\left(\displaystyle\sum_{n=0}^{s-1} \frac{(\lambda/\mu)^n}{n!}\right) + \frac{(\lambda/\mu)^s}{s!(1-(\lambda/s\mu))}} \tag{3.1}$$

- Probability of *exactly* n customers in the system: This equation has different forms dependent on n compared to the number of servers:

$$P_n = \begin{cases} \dfrac{(\lambda/\mu)^n}{n!}P_0 & \text{for } 0 \le n \le s \\ \dfrac{(\lambda/\mu)^n}{s!s^{n-s}}P_0 & \text{for } n \ge s \end{cases} \qquad (3.2)$$

- Probability that the number of customers in the system is equal to or greater than the number of servers (e.g., all the operators in a call center are busy):

$$P_{n \ge s} = \frac{(\lambda/\mu)^s}{s!(1-(\lambda/s\mu))}P_0. \qquad (3.3)$$

- The average number of customers in the system:

$$L = \frac{\lambda\mu(\lambda/\mu)^s}{(s-1)!(s\mu-\lambda)^2}P_0 + \frac{\lambda}{\mu},$$

or, alternatively,

$$L = \frac{(\lambda/\mu)^{s+1}}{s!s(1-(\lambda/s\mu))^2}P_0 + \frac{\lambda}{\mu}. \qquad (3.4)$$

- The average total time customers spend in the system:

$$W = L/\lambda = (L_q/\lambda) + (1/\mu).$$

- The average number of customers waiting in the queue (not yet being served):

$$L_q = L - (\lambda/\mu),$$

or, alternatively,

$$L_q = \frac{(\lambda/\mu)^{s+1}}{s!s(1-(\lambda/s\mu))^2}P_0. \qquad (3.5)$$

- The average time customers wait in the queue before being served:

$$W_q = L_q/\lambda.$$

Now, let us examine these expressions. First, we consider the case where s = 1. This is the M/M/1 model. Do the equations reduce down to the equations given in chapter 2 for the M/M/1 model? Because they should, this is a good check for both typographical errors when using the multiple-channel equations from your favorite reference and for validating your understanding of what the more advanced mathematical notation signifies.

My classroom experiences indicate that it would be useful to review some mathematical notation to save you the time of looking it up for yourself.

The exclamation point indicates a factorial expression, where

$$n! = 1 \times 2 \times \ldots \times (n-1) \times n.$$

when $n = 0$, $n! = 1$. Any value raised to a power of zero is 1. For example, $(x-1)^0 = 1$.

The summation term $\sum_{i=0}^{n} x^i$ is shorthand notation for $x^0 + x^1 + x^2 + \ldots + x^{n+1} + x^n$, where i is a counter that represents the parameter range from 0 to n. Of course, $x^0 = 1$.

Returning now to the equations at hand, the key parameter that must be derived first is P_0 because its value is necessary to determine the other measures. Equation 3.1 can be a nasty piece of work with increasing chances of making a mathematical error when there are many servers to deal with. Likewise, determining L (Equation 3.4) also requires care. The equations for L and P_0 can be expressed differently using only the value for s and the ratio of λ/μ. This allows an easier computation and enables the creation of reference tables for P_0, L_q, and L for various combinations of λ/μ and s when using the M/M/s model. These tables are provided in appendix C.

The good news is that the expressions for queue length and waiting times are quite simple thanks to Little's Law.

The probability of just n customers in the system (Equation 3.2) is useful for determining how likely it is that one or more servers are idle. This helps later when scheduling workloads in a place like a grocery store because it gives you an estimate of the slack time available for servers, who may then, for example, help to restock shelves.

Another useful observation is that a service manager can obtain an estimate of the overall average waiting time per customer by merely tallying the number of customers who enter the business during some selected time interval and counting the number of customers in the business at the end of that time interval. By collecting this information for several selected time periods, say every 15 minutes during a typical business day, you can average the results to obtain estimates of L and λ. Hence, using Little's Law, $W = L/\lambda$. An example of this will be discussed in chapter 7.

Example 3.1. Coffee Shop With Two Servers

Let's return to the Ken's Caffeine Fix example in chapter 2. The coffee shop has an average arrival rate (λ) of 24 customers per hour and an average service rate (μ) of 1 customer every 2 minutes = 30 customers/ hour. Recall that the average time spent waiting to be served in that coffee shop was 8 minutes, which is much too long for the typical office worker desiring a cup of coffee on his or her break. The average line length was 3.2 customers.

One solution to reduce the waiting time is for the owner to hire another server to increase the overall service rate for the coffee shop. So, plugging in the values for two servers in Equation 3.1 for P_0, we should get

$$P_0 = \frac{1}{1 + (24/30) + \dfrac{(24/30)^2}{2(1 - (24/60))}} = 0.428571.$$

You may ask, "Is this value correct? We only doubled the number of servers, but P_0 has more than doubled compared to the M/M/1 model." The answer is yes, and it indicates that simply doubling the service rate of a single server is not the same as adding another server. This observation has important implications when deciding whether to hire another person or invest in service improvements (chapter 6). Table 3.1 compares the performance measure results for the M/M/1, M/M/2, M/M/1 with μ doubled, and M/M/1 with λ halved approaches. This will help illustrate why such simplified approaches, although they look like they would intuitively work, do not provide accurate answers.

Some readers may also ask, "Why are the answers expressed in so many significant digits?" In queuing analysis, particularly for the more complex models, it is important that you maintain as much precision as possible in the intermediate computations until you obtain the final result, which then can be rounded to a less detailed answer. Not doing this can have a noticeable effect on the final result. Not being aware of this creates considerable confusion for students who are doing homework together because when they compare their results, their answers often do not agree—leading them to assume that one of them has made a mistake.

Now that we have the value for P_0, we can determine the probability that just one server will be idle. Using Equation 3.2 for one server idle (i.e., $n = 1$ customer in the system), this is simply

$$\lambda P_0/\mu = \rho P_0 = 0.343.$$

Again, this is useful to know when considering how much of a new employee's time can be used for work not directly related to serving customers.

Determining the probability of more than 5 customers in the shop is much more complicated than the simple formula used for the M/M/1 model. Now we need to determine the respective probabilities of just 0, 1, 2, 3, 4, and 5 customers in the shop using Equation 3.2, add those values together, and then, recalling that the total of all possible probabilities must equal 1, subtract that sum from 1 to obtain the probability we seek. Without showing the intermediate calculations, the values in this example are $P_1 = 0.343$, $P_2 = 0.137$, $P_3 = 0.055$, $P_4 = 0.022$, and $P_5 = 0.009$. This gives a value for $P_{n>5} = 0.006$ or 0.6%, which is a large improvement over the 26.2% value for the M/M/1 model.

Now we consider our major concern, "How much did we reduce the average waiting time?" First, we need to calculate the average line length using Equation 3.4. Plugging in the numbers using the P_0 value determined earlier, we should get

$$L = \frac{(24/30)^3}{2! \times 2(1 - (24/60))^2} \times 0.428571 + \frac{24}{30} = 0.952381 \text{ customer.}$$

Dividing L by λ gives us a total average waiting time of 0.039682 hour, or roughly 2.4 minutes, which is a much more reasonable time to get a cup of coffee. The corresponding average length of the queue is now 0.152381 customer, and the average wait in line is less than a minute at 22.9 seconds.

Table 3.1. Comparison of the Results Using Correct Analysis Methods With the Results Using Incorrect Methods (Shaded Results)

	M/M/1	M/M/2	M/M/1 (2μ)	M/M/1 (λ/2)
P_0	0.2	0.428	0.600	0.600
L	4	0.952	0.667	0.667
L_q	3.2	0.152	0.267	0.267
W	10 minutes	2.38 minutes	3.33 minutes	1.67 minutes
W_q	8 minutes	0.38 minute	1.33 minutes	0.67 minute

Finally, let's return to the earlier comment about why one should not use the M/M/1 equations in chapter 2 for determining the enhanced performance provided by adding another server. Referring to Table 3.1, if one doubles the service rate using a single line, the average line appears to be shorter than the M/M/2 solution, but the average total wait is longer. If one assumes that customers will evenly split between separate lines for each server (i.e., halving the arrival rate), the average line length and the average total waiting time are both smaller than for the M/M/2 solution. What are the reasons for not being able to use the results in the shaded cells of Table 3.1?

As will be explored further in subsequent chapters, there are several subtle things going on here. One server working at an average of 30 seconds per customer is not the same as the combination of two servers each working at an average of 1 minute per customer. The average throughput is the same, but the combined variance in the service rate for two servers is not the same as the variance for a single server. In addition, the average service rate of 2μ is valid only when both servers are busy. When only one server is busy, the service rate is μ.

Referring to our discussion of state diagrams in chapter 1, let us change the situation from a single-channel system to a multiple-channel system with two servers. An example would be a call center with two operators and no ability to have callers on hold. The output from state 2 back to state 1 shown in Figure 1.3 would be 2μ for a two-server system. The set of expressions for Equation 1.3 would change to

$$\text{State 0: } (P_1 \times \mu) = (P_0 \times \lambda),$$
$$\text{State 1: } (P_0 \times \lambda) + (P_2 \times 2\mu) = (P_1 \times \lambda) + (P_1 \times \mu),$$
$$\text{State 2: } (P_1 \times \lambda) = (P_2 \times 2\mu).$$

Solving for P_0, P_1, and P_2 in the same manner as described in chapter 1, we obtain

$$P_0 = 1/[1 + \rho + (\rho^2/2)],$$
$$P_1 = \rho/[1 + \rho + (\rho^2/2)],$$
$$P_2 = (\rho^2/2)/[1 + \rho + (\rho^2/2)].$$

The results show a relative increase in the probabilities of states 0 and 1 and a corresponding decrease in the probability of state 2, as we should expect. Again, adding P_0, P_1, and P_2, we obtain a value of 1 as a check on our derivation.

When a customer enters a shop with two lines, the customer normally picks the shorter line, but he or she can pick the longer line if the customer perceives that the shorter line has a customer ahead in line that is likely to require a much longer service time (e.g., a person with a large number of packages at the post office).

Customers may change lines if the line they are in is moving slower than the other line. (We all have done this in slow-moving traffic when given an opportunity to move into a faster moving lane.) This behavior is called jockeying. The configuration of a single line feeding the next available server prevents jockeying and reduces the chances that a new customer will get stuck in a line behind a customer requiring a long service time.

You can divide the arrival rate *if* you add another server at a separate location so that the possibility of customers choosing or jockeying between the lines is eliminated. Then the two lines can be considered to be independent of each other, and each can be analyzed separately using the M/M/1 model equations. In such situations, the arrival rate for each location is determined by dividing the original total arrival rate according to what percentage you estimate will go to each location.

You can have an average total waiting time that is less than the average service time when the customer volume is low ($\rho < 0.5$) because the probability of a long service time delaying other customers is reduced. In effect, you are averaging the service time at one window with a customer with zero service time at the windows with no customers. In addition, when you use an exponential distribution to describe the range of possible service times, there is a cumulative probability that at least 63% of the possible service times will be shorter than the average service time.

Correspondingly, the cumulative probability for possible service times greater than the average service time is therefore 37%. If the service time can be more accurately represented with a normal distribution, such as businesses providing only standardized services, these cumulative probabilities would each be 50%.

CHAPTER 4

More Complex
Single-Channel Models

In many service businesses and manufacturing line applications, the basic M/M/1 model does not provide useful results that appear to agree with reality. There are several possible reasons for this poor performance:

- Chief and foremost, the waiting line formulas are based on the waiting line achieving a steady-state condition. This takes time and should lead you to the observation that the formulas are likely to be a poor predictor of what occurs at the beginning of a business day.
- The service time distribution is not best described by an exponential distribution.
- The capacity for accommodating the waiting line is limited.
- The calling population is not infinite.
- The interarrival time distribution is not best described by an exponential distribution.
- The M/M/1 model is based on a single-service phase, where the server performs all the service required. How do we handle situations where there is more than one phase or step? In some cases, we can combine the separate service steps to approximate a single phase. In others, we require either more complicated analysis approaches or simulations to obtain the performance data we want.

There are several adjustments we can make in the performance measures to cope with many of these situations. Some will work out well; others will give us only rough estimates of what is happening. In such cases, discrete simulation models may be the only way to gain more accurate insight into what is occurring. Some examples of simple simulations that can be done in Excel to analyze these situations are discussed in chapter 7.

Instead of the normal choice of an exponential distribution for the interarrival and service times, we have a variety of probability distributions that can be used to more accurately represent a particular service business situation. Some of these distributions will make the performance measures more complicated to determine. Some will require the use of simulations because of the lack of suitable, closed-form (analytical) solutions. The good news is that because Little's Law applies regardless of our choices for service and arrival distributions, all we have to be able to do is to calculate L, L_q, W, or W_q to determine the other values.

Alternate Service Time Distributions

The M/G/1 and M/D/1 models allow for other choices of service time distributions than the exponential distribution. Some common situations that require a different choice are when

- the minimum service time is significantly greater than the nearly zero times allowed by an exponential distribution;
- the service time may have a much smaller variance than allowed by the exponential distribution;
- the service time may even be consistent enough to be considered a constant value;
- the service time can have a discrete distribution, such as in the case of a business offering only a few standardized services;
- or the service time can be a collection of exponentially distributed service times, such as in the case of different classes of customers being served by the same facility.

Fortunately, we can obtain the steady-state average performance measures for many of these situations by using the Pollaczek-Khintchine (P-K) formula.[1] This formula uses the coefficient of variation (C_x) for a probability distribution of x to calculate the average waiting time in line (W_q). Because we are dealing only with the average steady-state value for the waiting time, the shape of the probability distribution used for the service time is unimportant as long as we know the distribution's mean value and standard deviation or variance. Here we assume that for an M/G/1 model, x represents the service time, and the mean service time is the reciprocal of the average service rate (μ):

$$W_q = \frac{1}{\mu} \times \frac{\lambda}{(\mu - \lambda)} \times \frac{\left(1 + C_{(1/\mu)}^2\right)}{2},$$

$$\text{where } C_{(1/\mu)} = \frac{\text{standard deviation}}{\text{mean}}.$$

(4.1)

Examine this formula carefully. For a constant service time where the standard deviation is zero, the time spent waiting in line is exactly half of what is predicted for the M/M/1 model using the same average service time.

You may very well say, "No service time is exactly constant where people are involved, what then?" In that case, we can use a normal distribution, where we collect samples of actual service times and calculate their average ($1/\mu$) and corresponding standard deviation (σ). This would give a $C_{(1/\mu)}$ value of $\mu\sigma$, and Equation 4.1 for a M/G/1 model using a normal service time distribution becomes

$$W_q = \frac{1}{\mu} \times \frac{\lambda}{(\mu - \lambda)} \times \frac{\left(1 + (\mu\sigma)^2\right)}{2} = \frac{\rho(1 + \mu^2\sigma^2)}{2(\mu - \lambda)}.$$

(4.2)

Let us examine this expression more closely. It says that as the variance in the service time increases, the wait becomes longer even though the average service time does not change.

Here is an important corollary: Reducing variances in the service time reduces the average waiting time. This corollary is important because most textbook examples focus on shortening the average service time to reduce the average waiting time. Some approaches for addressing service time variability are discussed in chapter 6.

What about the problem with the probability of unrealistically short service times using the exponential distribution? Unfortunately, the steady-state performance measures do not illustrate this problem; one must use simulation to see its effect. However, the subtle effects on average waiting time and line lengths can be taken into account by choosing general service time distributions that have a lower probability of shorter service times. In addition to the constant and normal distributions, we can use the Erlang probability density function, which is defined by the following formula:

$$f(t) = \frac{t^{k-1}e^{-t/\alpha}}{\alpha^k (k-1)!} \text{ for } 0 \leq t \leq \infty. \tag{4.3}$$

where α = the scale factor,[2] k = the shape factor, the mean = αk, and the variance = $\alpha^2 k$. In a gamma distribution, k is a continuous value; in an Erlang distribution, k is restricted to integer values greater than zero and, in essence, represents the number of identical but still indepen- dent exponential distributions that are added together to form the Erlang distribution. When k = 1, this distribution defaults to the exponential distribution, where the average time is α (substitute $1/\lambda$ for the interar- rival time and $1/\mu$ for the service time). This leads to another version of Equation 4.3 that is easier to understand when using it for service time distribution in $M/E_k/1$ models because it is expressed in terms of the ser- vice rate instead of α:

$$f(t) = \frac{\mu^k t^{k-1}e^{-\mu t}}{(k-1)!} \text{ for } 0 \leq t \leq \infty. \tag{4.4}$$

Therefore, the mean becomes k/μ, and the variance becomes k/μ^2. Plots of Equation 4.4 for an average service rate of 5 and using values of k = 1, 2, and 4 are shown in Figure 4.1. This service rate corresponds to an average service time of 0.2; while you may observe that the peak of the probability distribution for k = 2 roughly occurs at that time, that fact does not mean that the best value for k is 2. However, the mean for that curve is $k/\mu = 2/5 = 0.4$, indicating that there are a larger number of pos- sible times greater than the most probable time compared to the number of possible times less than the most probable time.

This illustrates a common area of confusion when trying to under- stand the mathematics behind the waiting line performance equations. My students often confuse the maximum value of a probability density function with the average they get from a collection of observations. They also forget that the Central Limit Theorem states that the distribution of sample averages is normally distributed regardless of the underlying distribution being sampled. I demonstrate to students that knowing the mean is not enough to determine which probability density function applies by giving them two sets of data that provide the same mean and

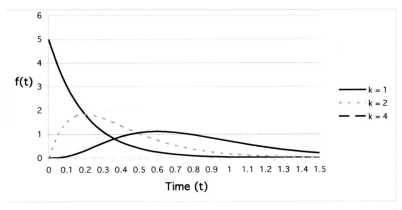

Figure 4.1. Probability density functions for an average service rate of 5 using an Erlang distribution with k = 1, 2, and 4.

standard deviation but show significantly different frequency distributions when the raw sample results are plotted in histograms.

So let us use the mean and variance for an Erlang distribution in the P-K formula given in Equation 4.1. In this case, $C_{(1/\mu)} = \dfrac{1}{\sqrt{k}}$, resulting in

$$W_q = \frac{1}{\mu} \times \frac{\lambda}{(\mu - \lambda)} \times \frac{\left(1 + (1/k)\right)}{2} = \frac{\rho(k+1)}{2k(\mu - \lambda)}. \qquad (4.5)$$

As a check, you can see that when k = 1, we obtain the same equation for an exponential distribution in the M/M/1 model. What if we try k = 2 to reduce the possibility of really short service times? Then using Equation 4.5, W_q = 75% of the W_q for the M/M/1 model. If the choice for k is much larger, we converge on the same result as for a constant service time.

How can this be? We have reduced the probability of short service times, so should the wait not be longer? This illustrates how our intuition is sometimes misleading when it comes to analyzing waiting lines. First, keep in mind that the exponential distribution was not representing realistic service times for Ken's Caffeine Fix, so comparing the new W_q to an incorrect W_q is inappropriate. Second, the higher k factor could have also reduced the probability of really long service times. What really matters is which service time distribution is the best representation of reality for a business like Ken's Caffeine Fix.

Example 4.1. Coffee Shop Using Different Service Distributions
Let us compare the differences in performance using different service distributions for Ken's Caffeine Fix analyzed in Example 2.1. The values for ρ and P_0 remain the same, but W_q, L_q, W, and L will vary. The average service rate of 30 customers per hour will be the same for all distributions, and we will assume a standard deviation of service time of 15 seconds for the normal distribution. Table 4.1 shows the results.

Table 4.1. Ken's Caffeine Fix Coffee Shop Performance Measures for Different Service Distributions With an Average Service Rate of 30 Customers per Hour

Performance	Exponential	Constant	Normal	Erlang (k = 2)
W_q (minutes)	8	4	3.05	4.5
W (minutes)	10	5	3.18	5.63
L_q (customers)	3.2	1.6	1.22	1.8
L (customers)	4	2	1.52	2.25

Observe that the best performance is with a normal service time distribution. Why is the constant service time not providing the best performance? Once again we must consider that when there is some variance in service time, we can have better results because there is a reasonable probability that the shorter service times will occur at the same time as when there is a higher than average arrival rate, enabling the line to move faster in such cases. Similarly, there is also a probability of longer service times occurring when the arrival rate is lower than normal, which will reduce their usual effect in increasing line lengths. The combination of these two possibilities results in slightly improved performance as long as the variance in service time is not too large. For example, if the standard deviation increases from 15 seconds to 30 seconds, W_q increases to 3.19 minutes, and L_q increases to 1.28 customers—as expected.

What about the beta distribution commonly used to represent completion times in project management planning? This asymmetrical distribution could be used because it allows the selection of a minimum time and the probability for much longer times. However, its mean and variance terms are much more complex compared to the choice of an

Erlang distribution with the proper value of k. In project management analysis, the beta distribution is often approximated by a normal distribution to simplify the mathematics. This approximation and its use for probabilistic estimates of project completion time can be found in many project management texts.

Finally, sometimes there is not enough information to determine what might be the best distribution to use. In such cases, we can take what operational data we do have regarding service times to form a discrete distribution that can be used in a simulation program. An example of this will be discussed in chapter 7.

Alternate Arrival Time Distributions

For most service business situations, the exponential distribution is a very good representation of customer arrival behavior. But, for some businesses, a better representation is needed. The Kendall notation for this situation using a single-channel, single-phase system is G/M/1:

- The arrival distribution may not be best represented by a Poisson distribution.
- Arrival rates can vary during the day and often have regularly occurring peak and slack periods depending on the nature of the service(s) provided.
- The arrival population could be a combination of different types of customers.

When appointments or production schedules are used to control the arrival rate, the notation is D/M/1. You may ask why we would want to use waiting line analysis for such a predictable situation. If we want to select the best time between successive appointments, it is necessary to evaluate the effects of varying service times. If the appointment duration is too short, we end the day with a long line of disgruntled customers still waiting to be served. If the appointment time is too long, we reduce the number of customers we can accommodate per day and will have more idle time than we can profitably use to do other tasks, such as cleanup, record keeping, and so forth. In other words, we must ensure that the average arrival rate is sufficiently lower than the average service rate to prevent unnecessary backups but not so low that we have reduced capacity and unnecessary idle time. Selecting the right value is a cost decision that we will discuss in chapter 6.

Dealing with varying arrival rates is difficult because the waiting line equations assume steady-state conditions. For small businesses, there is likely to be insufficient volume to achieve a steady-state situation each day. For businesses such as government driver's license bureaus or the post office, where the customer really does not have a choice of an alternate supplier, you can average the arrivals during the day to determine the level of service required. For businesses such as Ken's Caffeine Fix, staffing has to better match the ebb and flow of customers to provide acceptable service for customers who are not as tolerant of long lines and waiting times.

In both cases, but more so for Ken's and places like banks and grocery stores, it is important to have staff that can perform other business tasks when customer arrival volume is low. Knowing how much time is required for those tasks and the estimate of P_0 from the queuing analysis can provide guidance as to the total staffing needed.

Many businesses have collected point-of-sale data regarding the nature of the services they provide and the types of customers. Such data can be used to improve waiting line performance in several ways, particularly when more than one server is available, as will be discussed in more detail in chapter 5. For single server operations, this information can be used to ensure that adequate supplies are available for the different services requested by customers and help identify those parts of the service that might be delegated to some of the customers. For example, a coffee shop, noting that about 30% of its customers want a cup of house coffee only, could set up a self-serve station for those customers so that customers wanting more complex coffee mixtures could be served more quickly.

In factory applications, manufacturing custom or semicustom products creates different classes of arrivals. Another application where different classes of customers are likely is the machine repair model discussed later in this chapter when we cover the limited calling population model.

From an analysis viewpoint, it is relatively easy to combine separate classes of customers if the arrival behavior of each class can be described by a separate exponential distribution. In this case, the average arrival rate for the total distribution is just the sum of the individual average arrival rates. That is, $\lambda_{total} = \lambda_1 + \lambda_2 + \lambda_3 + \ldots$. Similarly, a total exponential distribution can be separated into individual exponential distributions according to their probability of occurrence.

Finally, there is one common arrival scenario that is difficult to classify, let alone analyze. Consider the restaurant situation where there is the usual exponential arrival of individual customers combined with regularly scheduled arrivals who have made reservations. So how does the restaurant handle a tour bus unloading a large group of passengers for lunch or dinner? Does the restaurant mix them in with individual customers or do they treat the group separately? What if the tour bus stops are unscheduled?

A closed-form solution does not exist for many of these arrival situations, and those that have been developed for very special situations are beyond the mathematical scope covered by this monograph. What we can do here is to attempt to break such a situation into separate parts that can be analyzed individually. For example, in the restaurant scenario, management could choose to require that groups above a certain size make a reservation to be served—in essence, creating two separate service operations that could be analyzed independently.

Limited Capacity

There can be physical limits on how many customers may be in line. This may take the form of how many customers can be accommodated on hold when a single operator at a call center is busy or when there is not enough room to accommodate a long line in a small shop. The Kendall notation for this situation is M/M/1/K/∞/FCFS, where K is the maximum number of people in a queue, including the customers being served at the moment. A specific example of this model was analyzed by the state diagram discussed in chapter 1 and shown in Figure 1.3. In that example, the value for K was two customers.

The performance measures for an M/M/1/K model are similar to those for the M/M/1 model but with slight modifications to account for a system capacity of K customers:

- Utilization factor: $\rho = \lambda/\mu$; for a M/M/1/K model, ρ must be ≤ 1
- Probability of zero customers in the system: $P_0 = (1 - \rho)/(1 - \rho^{K+1})$ for $\lambda < \mu$ and $P_0 = 1/(1 + K)$ for $\lambda = \mu$

- Probability of exactly n customers in the system: $P_n = P_0 \rho^n$ for $n \le K$
- Probability that the server is busy: $P_{n>0} = 1 - P_0 = \rho$
- Probability that a customer will be turned away: $P_K = P_0 \rho^K$
- Average number of customers in the system: $L = K/2$ for $\lambda = \mu$ and

$$L = \frac{\rho}{(1-\rho)} - \frac{(K+1)\rho^{(K+1)}}{\left(1 - \rho^{(K+1)}\right)} \text{ for } \lambda < \mu \qquad (4.6)$$

- Effective arrival rate: $\lambda' = \lambda(1 - P_K)$
- Average total time customers spend in the system: $W = L/\lambda' = L/(\lambda(1 - P_K))$
- Average number of customers waiting in the queue (not yet being served): $L_q = L - (\lambda'/\mu) = L - (\lambda(1 - P_K)/\mu) = \lambda' W_q$
- Average time customers wait in the queue before being served: $W_q = W - (1/\mu) = L_q/\lambda' = L_q/(\lambda(1 - P_K))$

Recall that for Little's Law, we need to use an effective arrival rate (λ'), which is the arrival rate multiplied by the probability of acceptance (1 minus the probability of the maximum number of customers allowed by the capacity limit). There are three possible assumptions here: (1) We lose the customers who are turned away because they have alternate service choices with our competitors, (2) those customers return later to try again as would be the case for a call center where they have no other choice for the support they want, or (3) the blocked customers give up trying.

Because we lose some customers in the first assumption or can smooth out peak arrival rates for the second assumption by forcing customers to call back again later, we can allow the average arrival rate to be as high as the average service rate, which explains the conditional equations for P_0 and L.

P_K gives us a value for lost business that can be used to compare with the cost of adding additional line capacity. P_K is sometimes called the blocking probability.

The astute reader may notice that the equation given for P_0 when $K = 2$ is not the same as the state diagram equation derived for P_0 in chapter 1. Let us compare them:

$$\text{Does } 1/(1 + \rho + \rho^2) = (1 - \rho)/(1 - \rho^3)?$$

Multiplying both sides by the denominators to remove the fractions, we get

$$1 - \rho^3 = (1 - \rho)(1 + \rho + \rho^2) = 1 + \rho + \rho^2 - \rho - \rho^2 - \rho^3 = 1 - \rho^3.$$

Okay, they match! (Before I get too cocky, maybe we should also check the respective equations for L just to be sure.)

Once we have the probability for each state in Figure 1.3, we can determine the average number of persons in the system by multiplying the number of persons represented by each state by that state's probability. That is, $L = (P_0 \times 0) + (P_1 \times 1) + (P_2 \times 2)$ for the state diagram in Figure 1.3, which gives $L = (\rho + 2\rho^2)/(1 + \rho + \rho^2)$. Does that equate to the expression in Equation 4.6 when $K = 2$? That is, does $(\rho + 2\rho^2)/(1 + \rho + \rho^2) = [\rho/(1 - \rho)] - [3\rho^3/(1 - \rho^3)]$?

Multiplying both sides by the denominators to remove the fractions and then combining the terms on both sides, we can see that the two expressions do equate to the same value.

It is suggested that you do this check for yourself as practice in verifying formulas. When there are several terms with subscripts and superscripts, it is easy for typographical errors to occur. Verifying equations and making sure that the units of measure cancel out to the desired set of units are methods for detecting many typographical errors.

Example 4.2. Coffee Shop With Limited Capacity

Returning to Ken's Caffeine Fix, the owner is concerned that the shop is turning away customers because the maximum customer capacity is 7 customers. Using the same arrival rate of 24/hour, a service rate of 30/hour, and a capacity $K = 7$, we determine P_0 to be $(1 - 0.8)/(1 - 0.8^8) = 0.240319$. Compare this value with the 20% value obtained for P_0 in chapter 2; you can see that the loss of customers turned away has increased the probability of idle time.

To determine the percentage of customers lost, we need to determine the value for $P_K = P_0\rho^K = 0.240319 \times 0.8^7 = 0.050398 = 5\%$. This loss creates an effective arrival rate $\lambda' = 24 \times (1 - P_K) = 22.8/$hour, and the average line length $L = 4$ from chapter 2 is reduced using Equation 4.6 to $4 - [(8 \times 0.8^8)/(1 - 0.8^8)] = 2.39$ customers. The total wait in the system has been reduced from 10 minutes to $2.39/22.8 = 0.1048$ hours $= 6.29$ minutes.

The lesson to be learned here is that customers lost because of capacity limitations are not often noticed because the line is longest at those times when the server is busiest. This also results in the average line length and overall waiting time being shorter, creating an illusion that the service is being performed more efficiently than it is. A 5% customer loss may not seem to be that significant, but when you compare its lost revenue with the profit margin for many small service businesses. . . .

Limited Calling Population

The available customer population may be limited, as in the case for a service operation maintaining a fleet of airplanes for a major airline or a group servicing the copiers at a company. The Kendall notation for this situation when there is only one server is $M/M/1/\infty/N/FCFS$, where N represents the number of customers or items to be served. In many textbooks and articles, this situation is often referred to as the machine repairman problem.

Because the costs of downtime can be quite high, there are often two or more servers. This complicates the closed-form solutions considerably. This situation will be discussed in much more detail in chapter 5. Here, we will discuss the single-server model because it provides some insight into the fundamental issues involved and is appropriate for many small service operations responsible for maintaining and repairing a small set of equipment. This also applies to those operations where one professional serves a select group of customers.

The arrival rate for a repair operation supporting N machines is usually dictated by three things: the recommended preventive maintenance period, the expected failure rate, and the equipment usage rate (supplies replenishment). Equivalents of these rate components also apply to handling a select group of clients, such as at a financial advisor brokerage: regularly scheduled status appointments, typical percentage of emergency consultations, and volume-related requests.

We can attempt to analyze these classes as one combined calling population, or we can assign separate servers for each class. Consider that the preventive maintenance arrivals are essentially appointment based, and their respective service times are likely to be relatively constant or at least normally distributed with small standard deviations. The failure rate and subsequent repair times are more likely to be described by exponential distributions.

The base arrival rate for an M/M/1/∞/N model is defined by the needs of one customer, item, or machine for the situation under consideration. In the case of a machine, it can be the expected time between repairs or scheduled maintenance. The effective arrival rate is the basic arrival rate per unit λ_u multiplied by the number of units (N – L) in the finite population N that are not currently in line for service in the system. The calculations for P_0 with a finite population of N customers (machines) are considerably nastier because now we have to account for the reduced probability of future arrivals as current arrivals enter the system and are taken care of. This requires using N summation terms, as shown in the following set of performance measures:

- Effective arrival rate: $\lambda' = \lambda_u(N - L)$
- Unit utilization factor $\rho_u = \lambda_u/\mu$
- Probability of zero customers in the system:

$$P_0 = \frac{1}{\sum_{n=0}^{N}\left[\dfrac{N!}{(N-n)!} \times \rho_u^n\right]} \quad (4.7)$$

- Probability of exactly n customers in the system:

$$P_n = P_0 \times \left[\frac{N!}{(N-n)!} \times \rho_u^n\right] \text{ for } n \leq N; \ P_n = 0 \text{ for } n > N$$

- Average number of customers waiting in the queue (not yet being served):

$$L_q = N - \left[\left(\frac{\lambda_u + \mu}{\lambda_u}\right)(1 - P_0)\right]$$

- Average number of customers in the system: $L = L_q + (1 - P_0)$
- Average time customers wait in the queue before being served:

$$W_q = L_q/(\lambda_u(N - L))$$

- Average total time customers spend in the system:

$$W = W_q + (1/\mu) = L/(\lambda_u(N - L))$$

Looking at the equation for P_0, it increases in value as N becomes smaller, which is what we would expect with a lighter workload. However, as N becomes larger, there will be many terms in the denominator. This leads some of my business students to ask the question, "How large would N have to be where we could assume that an infinite calling population model could give us a ballpark estimate with only a small percentage of error? The calculations would certainly be easier to do."

If we attempt to do this, I remind them that we must recognize that we are not dealing with the same definition of arrival rate. In a repair service situation, the average arrival rate is based on some expected rate of failure per unit; as the number of possible items to be repaired increases, the effective arrival rate increases. The $M/M/1/\infty/N$ model takes these increases in N into account in its performance measures, but an $M/M/1/\infty/\infty$ model assumes an average arrival rate that is independent of population size.

Example 4.3. Repair Service With One Server

Consider an in-house service activity staffed with a single person. Campus Reboot is responsible for maintaining a set of network printers located in several buildings clustered together as part of a liberal arts college. Campus Reboot is only responsible for repairs because routine reloading of paper, installing new toner cartridges, and clearing simple paper jams are done when needed by the respective department secretaries. At the moment, there are only 10 of these printers in use, but their popularity with the faculty for printing exams and quizzes is increasing, and the dean of the college wants to know what effect increasing the number of printers to 25 or even 50 units will have on the repair response. For now, we will ignore the associated costs but will return to this example in chapter 6 to discuss the cost trade-offs. The failure rate for the current printer model used is 250 hours between repairs, and the typical repair takes an average of 4 hours, which includes any time spent to order parts or travel between buildings. This information converts into an arrival rate λ_u per printer of $1/250 = 0.004$ printer/hour and an average service rate of 0.25 printer/hour. This results in a value for $\rho_u = 0.004/0.25 = 0.016$.

There is an important consideration to note here. Some of you may be tempted to multiply the arrival rate per item by the total number of items to obtain the average arrival rate for λ. *Do not* do this because the derivation of the equations is based on the arrival rate per unit, which I designate by λ_u to avoid confusion with the more common understanding of what λ represents.

For example, consider the state diagram for a population of four items, as shown in Figure 4.2, where each state indicated by the hexagons represents the number of items L in the system. The arrival rate from state 0 to state 1 is $4\lambda_u$ because the entire population is available to move to that state. Similarly, the number of items available to move from state 3 to state 4 is only one because all the other items in the population are already in the system. The rate for moving the other direction, reducing the number of items in the system, is the service rate, which can be applied to only one item at a time. If there are 2 servers instead of 1 server, then the reduction rate is 2μ from states 2, 3, and 4 and μ from state 1.

If you use Excel to determine P_0, I recommend having separate columns as shown in Figure 4.3, for the terms in the summation portion of the denominator of Equation 4.7: n, $(\rho_u)^n$, $(N - n)!$, and the product within the brackets, rather than attempting to compose a single expression to calculate P_0. Using N as an input value and summing the column for the products allows a simpler algorithm for computing the final result. This helps minimize computation errors, which is critically important for P_0 because it is used for subsequent calculations. It also allows for easy expansion to larger N values by using Excel's AutoFill capability to copy the respective formulas in each column further down the sheet.

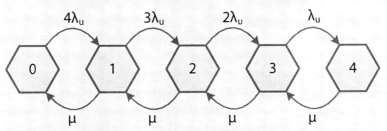

Figure 4.2. State diagram for a single-server system with a limited population of four items with individual arrival rates of λ_u.

Table 4.2. Performance Measures for M/M/∞/N Model With N = 10, 25, and 50 Units Using the Input Data for Campus Reboot From Example 4.3

N	10	25	50
P_0	0.842919	0.609848	0.242301
L_q	0.025346	0.225374	1.886103
L	0.182427	0.615525	2.643802
λ'	0.0392702	0.0975379	0.1894248
W_q (hours)	0.645432	2.310626	9.957002
W (hours)	4.645432	6.310626	13.957

Table 4.2 summarizes the results for repair populations of 10, 25, and 50 printers in response to the dean's request regarding the effect of adding more printers to Campus Reboot's repair response. With 10 printers, the average wait before repair work begins is about 39 minutes. This average waiting time increases to about 2.3 hours for 25 printers and nearly 10 hours for 50 printers. The number of printers

Figure 4.3. Excel setup to determine P_0 (shaded cell at upper right) and P_n for Example 4.3 with a population of 10 network printers. P_0 is the inverse of the sum of the products, and the other P_ns are the respective product for n multiplied by the value for P_0. As a check on the accuracy of the computations, the sum of the probabilities is 1.0.

n	(N − n)!	N!/(N − n)!	$(\rho_u)^n$	Product	P_n
0	3628800	1	1	1	0.842919
1	362880	10	0.016	0.16	0.134867
2	40320	90	0.000256	0.02304	0.019421
3	5040	720	4.1E-06	0.002949	0.002486
4	720	5040	6.55E-08	0.00033	0.000278
5	120	30240	1.05E-09	3.17E-05	2.67E-05
6	24	151200	1.68E-11	2.54E-06	2.14E-06
7	6	604800	2.68E-13	1.62E-07	1.37E-07
8	2	1814400	4.29E-15	7.79E-09	6.57E-09
9	1	3628800	6.87E-17	2.49E-10	2.1E-10
10	1	3628800	1.1E-18	3.99E-12	3.36E-12
			Sum	1.186354	1

awaiting repair increases from the current value of 0.025 printer to nearly 2 printers for a 50-printer population.

Reviewing the results in Figure 4.3, the likelihood of more than 1 printer awaiting repair (2 or more printers total in the repair shop) by Campus Reboot is less than $(1 - P_0 - P_1) = 0.022214 = 2.22\%$ for the current population of 10 printers.

If Campus Reboot works only a normal 8-hour day, it is likely that it will often take more than 2 days before some departments get back their broken printer if the number of printers increases to 50. This would be unacceptable given that a normal exam week is only 5 days long. We will return to this example in chapter 5 to determine the effect of adding another repair person to Campus Reboot's staff.

It should be noted here that many college textbooks still use lookup tables to solve this type of example for both single-channel and multiple-channel situations. As a result, the equations presented by those authors do not look anything like the equations used here. Instead, they use terms and expressions that work with these tables, often referred to in some textbooks as finite queuing tables (to be more correct some authors use the terms finite queuing for limited capacity models and finite sourcing for limited calling population models, which applies here). An example is the service factor X = average service (repair) time T divided by the sum of the average repair time T and the average time between repairs U. For Example 4.3, Campus Reboot's service factor would be $4/(250 + 4) = 0.0157$. The finite sourcing table for a given repair population level provides two variables, D and F, for each combination of X and number of servers. Using these variables, one then can determine the usual performance measures.

Such methods are a product of an earlier time when personal computers and spreadsheet programs were not yet available. At that time, calculations like those shown in Figure 4.3 using pencil-and-paper methods were tedious, time-consuming, and more prone to errors. This led to the development of lookup tables for various values of N, service factors, and the number of servers (repair persons) to expedite such analysis. Often-quoted examples of finite sourcing tables in college textbooks are sample tables for N = 5 or 10 used with permission from the 1958 reference published by Peck and Hazelwood.[3]

In this monograph readers are encouraged to use Excel-based methods because they allow a wider range of choices and conditions to best suit a given business situation. Instead of providing lookup tables, the equations for their creation are provided. Readers wishing more details regarding the derivation of these equations are encouraged to consult the excellent books by Hillier and Lieberman (2010) or Laguna and Marklund (2005).

Multiple Phases

In factory applications and some service businesses, there is more than one step (phase) in the process. How do we deal with those cases? Because each phase is likely to have a different service rate distribution, a closed-form generic solution would be unwieldy, even if the solution were possible. Some references are provided for those who are interested in pursuing closed-form solutions when they are available. *A cautionary note is appropriate here.* Many of the analytical solutions involve some in-depth mathematics and statistics understanding to determine whether they are appropriate for your business situation.

What if you do not want to become a math whiz to obtain some insight into how a multiple-phase process works? Not to fear, there are some characteristics we can work with to gain some understanding about such processes without the need for complex mathematics.

- The average arrival rate into each phase will be the same, assuming no losses or additions at each phase, because what went into the previous phase must come out of that phase.
- If losses or additions do occur during the process, they can be handled if we know their percentage related to the initial input arrival rate.
- In the case of factory applications, we usually have control over the arrival rate distribution by using production scheduling.
- Each phase can have a different service rate without affecting the average arrival rates into each phase.

Given these conditions, we can analyze or simulate a production process as a sequence of single-channel, single-phase waiting lines with the output of the preceding phase becoming the input to the following phase.

Because we can also accommodate a mixture of multiple-channel, single-phase process steps in manufacturing to deal with bottleneck capacity issues, there is a more detailed discussion of multiple-phase applications in chapter 7.

CHAPTER 5

More Complex
Multiple-Channel Models

In many service businesses and manufacturing line applications, the basic M/M/s model, like the M/M/1 model discussed in chapter 4, does not always provide useful results that appear to agree with reality. In addition to the reasons listed at the beginning of chapter 4, there are added factors as a result of using more than one server:

- More complex formulas to deal with, particularly for situations with limited queues or limited calling populations
- The opportunity to separate customers into different classes
- The opportunity to treat customers with different priorities
- The effects of using different line configurations
- Server capability differences

Equations 3.1 through 3.5 for the basic M/M/s model are restated here in a different form using ρ instead of λ/μ.[1] This allows for easier computation of basic performance values.

$$P_0 = \frac{1}{\left(\sum_{n=0}^{s-1} \frac{\rho^n}{n!}\right) + \frac{\rho^s}{s!(1-\rho/s)}}, \qquad (5.1)$$

$$P_n = \begin{cases} \dfrac{\rho^n}{n!} P_0 & \text{for } 0 \le n \le s \\[2mm] \dfrac{\rho^n}{s!\,s^{n-s}} P_0 & \text{for } n \ge s \end{cases}, \qquad (5.2)$$

$$P_{n \ge s} = \frac{\rho^s}{s!(1-\rho/s)} P_0, \qquad (5.3)$$

$$L = \frac{\rho^{s+1}}{s!s(1-\rho/s)^2} P_0 + \rho, \tag{5.4}$$

and

$$L_q = \frac{\rho^{s+1}}{s!s(1-\rho/s)^2} P_0 = L - \rho. \tag{5.5}$$

The time spent waiting in line and the total time in the system can be easily determined for a given average arrival rate using Little's Law after you have calculated the number of customers in line and in the system. The data tables in appendix C provide the values of P_0, L_q, and L for various combinations of ρ values and number of servers up to 10. You are encouraged to set up your own spreadsheet to do these calculations for values of ρ not listed and/or larger numbers of servers.

Looking at the values listed in appendix C, one can observe that as ρ approaches a value equal to the number of servers chosen, the length of the queue rapidly increases. The implication is, like the situation for a single-channel model, to not plan for an overall utilization factor, ρ/s, greater than 90% if you want to have some reserve capacity for unexpected increases in the average customer arrival rate. Also, the tables do not list values for every combination of ρ and number of servers because I have arbitrarily limited the values to what I consider to be practical solutions. For example, having more than 3 servers for $\rho < 1$ would be a waste of resources in most situations.

Looking at the values of L, some of my business students ask why one would want to plan for fewer customers in the system than the number of servers available. I remind them that the L values are a steady-state average over time, but there will often be clusters of customers arriving within a limited period in a real-life situation. Without some reserve capacity, the customer wait at those times can be unacceptably long. The managerial view here is to have servers whose skills are flexible enough so that they can do other things for the business when the number of customers is sparse. Businesses that are good at this are grocery stores, banks, and the post office—either calling staff to the checkout lines when business is heavy or training employees to open another service window when a customer line reaches a specified length.

Limited Capacity

This situation using multiple-channel models is often applied to call centers where the number of people who can be put on hold awaiting the next available representative is limited. When that capacity is filled with waiting customers, new customers encounter a busy signal and in effect are *blocked* from entering the system. Estimating how many customers are being turned away is necessary to determine how many representatives (and phone lines) are needed to provide a desired level of service (the percentage of customers who do not encounter busy signals; that is, those not blocked from entering the system).

When the number of customers is equal to the number of servers, there are no customers waiting in line. This condition occurred in the early days of queuing theory when the most common application was telephone exchanges using operators to make connections for callers. The technology for allowing customers to wait in an electronic line was not yet developed, and callers got a busy signal if the operators were already engaged with helping previous callers. Such queuing models were called an *Erlang loss system* because potential customers were lost when all the servers were busy. When a waiting line application allowed customers waiting for service to form a line, it was then called an *Erlang delay system* because those customers were not lost when all the servers were busy; they were just delayed in receiving service.

The set of average performance equations for the M/M/s/K model with a system capacity of K customers is as follows (K must be $\geq$ s):

- Utilization factors (note that ρ can be greater than 1 if the number of servers is greater than 1):

$$\rho_s = \lambda/s\mu$$
$$\rho = \lambda/\mu$$

- Probability of zero customers in the system:

$$P_0 = \frac{1}{\sum_{n=0}^{s} \frac{\rho^n}{n!} + \frac{\rho^s}{s!} \sum_{n=s+1}^{K} \rho^{n-s}} \tag{5.6}$$

- Probability of exactly n customers in the system:

$$P_n = \begin{cases} \dfrac{\rho^n}{n!}P_0 & \text{for } 0 \le n \le s \\[2ex] \dfrac{\rho^n}{s!s^{n-s}}P_0 & \text{for } s \le n \le K \\[2ex] 0 & \text{for } n > K \end{cases} \tag{5.7}$$

- Probability of customers in the system greater than the number of servers (probability that the servers are busy):

$$P_{n>s} = 1 - P_0 \sum_{n=0}^{s} \frac{\rho^n}{n!}$$

- Probability that a customer will be turned away: $P_K = P_0\rho^K/s!s^{K-s}$
- Average number of customers waiting in the queue (not yet being served):

$$L_q = \frac{P_0\rho^{s+1}}{s!s\left(1 - \dfrac{\rho}{s}\right)^2}\left\{1 - \left[1 + (K-s)\left(1 - \frac{\rho}{s}\right)\right]\left(\frac{\rho}{s}\right)^{K-s}\right\} \tag{5.8}$$

There is no solution in Equation 5.8 when $\rho_s = \rho/s = 1$. A solution can be found using L'Hospital's Rule[2] twice to obtain the limit for L_q when ρ/s approaches the value of 1. Although the resulting numerator terms can be complex, the denominator term reduces to $2s!s$ for $\rho/s = 1$.

- Average number of customers in the system:

$$L = L_q + \sum_{n=0}^{s-1} nP_n + s\left(1 - \sum_{n=0}^{s-1} P_n\right) \tag{5.9}$$

- Effective arrival rate: $\lambda' = \lambda(1 - P_K)$
- Average total time customers spend in the system: $W = L/\lambda' = L/(\lambda(1 - P_K))$
- Average time customers wait in the queue before being served:

$$W_q = L_q/\lambda' = L_q/(\lambda(1 - P_K))$$

Like the discussion in chapter 4 for the M/M/1 model, we need to use an effective arrival rate (λ') for Little's Law. This is the arrival rate minus the customers or items turned away by the limit in line capacity. The assumption is that those customers are lost and do not return. Because we lose some customers, we can allow the average arrival rate to be as high as the average service rate, which explains the conditional equations for P_n expressed by Equation 5.7. P_K gives us a value for lost business that can be used to compare with the cost of adding additional line capacity. P_K is sometimes called the blocking probability.

Limited Calling Population

Example 4.3 described a repair service with one person responsible for maintaining 10 items. When the number of customers or items becomes significantly larger, as illustrated in that example, more than one person is usually needed to provide an adequate turnaround time for items needing repair or maintenance. There are two approaches for analyzing the performance of adding staff:

1. If an item requiring service is of the type where a service crew can be effectively used (such as maintenance on an airplane or a truck), then the repair crew is treated as a single server where adding a member to the crew hopefully reduces the average service time per item. In this case, the M/M/1/∞/N model discussed in chapter 4 would still apply, but we would use a shorter repair time associated with the increased crew staff for our calculations.

2. However, in many repair and maintenance situations, the item requiring service can be effectively worked on by only one person. Hence, we need to use the M/M/s/∞/N model to determine the average performance expected if we decide to add one or more servers to improve performance. The disadvantage is that the equations become much more challenging to use, and additional care is required to avoid mathematical errors.

Recalling the use of an unit arrival rate and associated unit utilization factor as discussed for the single-channel limited population model in chapter 4, the set of average performance equations for the M/M/s/∞/N model with a limited population of N customers or items to be served is as follows (N must be ≥ s):

- Arrival rate per unit in the population: λ_u
- Unit utilization factor: $\rho_u = \lambda_u/\mu$
- Probability of zero customers in the system:

$$P_0 = \frac{1}{\left(\sum_{n=0}^{s-1} \frac{N!\rho_u^n}{(N-n)!n!}\right) + \sum_{n=s}^{N} \frac{N!\rho_u^n}{(N-n)!s!s^{n-s}}} \qquad (5.10)$$

- Probability of exactly n customers in the system:

$$P_n = \begin{cases} \dfrac{N!\rho_u^n}{(N-n)!n!}P_0 & \text{for } 0 \leq n \leq s \\[2ex] \dfrac{N!\rho_u^n}{(N-n)!s!s^{n-s}}P_0 & \text{for } s \leq n \leq N \\[2ex] 0 & \text{for } n > N \end{cases}$$

- Probability of customers in the system equal to or greater than the number of servers (probability that the servers are busy):

$$P_{n>s} = 1 - P_0 \sum_{n=0}^{s} \frac{N!\rho_u^n}{(N-n)!n!}$$

- Average number of customers waiting in the queue (not yet being served):

$$L_q = \sum_{n-s}^{N} (n-s)P_n \qquad (5.12)$$

- Average number of customers in the system:

$$L = L_q + \sum_{n=0}^{s-1} nP_n + s\left(1 - \sum_{n=0}^{s-1} P_n\right) \qquad (5.13)$$

- Effective arrival rate: $\lambda' = \lambda_u (N - L)$
- Average total time customers spend in the system: $W = L/\lambda' = L/(\lambda_u (N - L))$
- Average time customers wait in the queue before being served:

$$W_q = L_q/\lambda' = L_q/(\lambda_u(N - L))$$

- Probability of no waiting time for the next arrival:

$$P(W_q = 0) = \sum_{0}^{s-1} P_n$$

Before returning to Example 4.3 to see what improvement is possible for a greater number of printers by adding staff, let us consider how we might develop our own finite queuing tables[3] using Equations 5.10 through 5.13 in a spreadsheet program like Excel. Like the multiple-server table in appendix C, we can obtain some useful values of P_0, L_q, and L for various combinations of N, ρ, and s. Like the finite queuing tables published by Peck and Hazelwood (1958), it will be best if we prepare separate tables for different calling population sizes. But unlike Peck and Hazelwood's tables, we can set up our Excel solutions so that we can obtain P_0, L_q, and L directly rather than going through the use of some intermediary variables.

Unlike the equations provided in chapter 3 for the basic M/M/s model, the equations for P_0, L_q, and L become too complicated to formulate in a single Excel cell when the population is limited because of the extensive summations required in the formulas. Therefore, if you want to set up your own set of tables, you will need to use some additional columns to compute the summation values for specific combinations of ρ_u and s for your specific population N. Recall that we did this in chapter 4 when we analyzed a single-channel model with a limited line capacity K (see Figure 4.3).

An example spreadsheet solution is illustrated in appendix C for Example 5.1, where we return to the Campus Reboot situation discussed in chapter 4 and consider adding one or more servers to that repair service.

Example 5.1. Repair Service with Multiple Servers

Returning to the Campus Reboot service example in chapter 4, we recall that the service response would become unacceptable if we added 25 or 50 printers. So the dean has asked us how much improvement we would obtain if we hired another repair person or two. Using the equations just given for the M/M/s/∞/N model, we obtain the values shown in Table 5.1. Appendix C shows a copy of the Excel spreadsheet for the N = 10, s = 3 situation. Like the Excel setup shown in Figure 4.3, it is useful to set up separate columns for the summation terms required. Once those columns are established, it is easy to add additional terms for larger values of N by just copying the formulas down the sheet for each value of 0 to N. These columns also allow easier troubleshooting for mathematical errors.

Table 5.1. Performance Measures for M/M/s/∞/N Model with N = 10, 25, and 50 Units Using 1, 2, or 3 Servers for Example 5.1

N	10 Printers			25 Printers			50 Printers		
Servers	s = 1	s = 2	s = 3	s = 1	s = 2	s = 3	s = 1	s = 2	s = 3
P_0	0.842	0.853	0.853	0.609	0.669	0.672	0.242	0.434	0.450
L_q	0.025	0.001	0.000	0.225	0.014	0.001	1.886	0.131	0.016
L	0.182	0.158	0.158	0.616	0.407	0.395	2.644	0.917	0.803
λ'	0.039	0.040	0.040	0.098	0.098	0.098	0.189	0.196	0.197
W_q (hours)	0.645	0.018	0.001	2.311	0.141	0.010	9.957	0.669	0.080
W (hours)	4.645	4.018	4.001	6.311	4.141	4.010	13.95	4.669	4.080

As a check for mathematical errors, several conditions can be observed to indicate whether or not they are present. If these conditions are not present, then it is very likely that you have made either a mathematical error or incorrectly typed in a cell reference. Check the following:

- Is the waiting time in the system at least equal to the repair time for the item in question? For Example 5.1, it is four hours per printer.
- Does P_0 increase in diminishing increments as the number of servers increases for a given value of N?
- Do L_q and L decrease in diminishing increments as the number of servers increases for a given value of N?
- Does λ' increase as the number of servers increases (minor change) and with increases in N (bigger change)?
- Is the sum of all the Π_n's 1.000? Given the numerical precision used in your calculations, the result could be off a significant digit or two, but it must be very close to 1.000.

Observing the results in Table 5.1, my initial conclusion would recommend staying with one server for the current population of 10 printers and using 2 servers for the populations of 25 printers and

50 printers. This recommendation would provide roughly equivalent turnaround performance for all populations. It should also be noted that with a population of 50 printers, it is more likely that a faculty member can find an alternate printer to use temporarily when his or her usual printer is being repaired. This possibility would support not adding a third server for the 50-printer situation.

To obtain a full analysis for a more informed recommendation, we need to consider the trade-offs in the costs of hiring another repair person versus having a faculty member wait longer for a repair to be completed.

Different Classes of Customers

An important consideration in improving service performance when working with multiple-channel waiting lines is recognizing whether or not you have different classes of customers *with* different service distributions. When more than one server is required to provide acceptable service, an added decision is whether you have each server handle any customer that arrives or designate servers to specific classes of customers. A common example is the use of express and regular checkout lines at a grocery store when the store is large enough to justify having more than one checkout clerk.

More detailed aspects about taking advantage of customer classes for improving service performance is discussed in chapter 6, where we also can take into account other managerial considerations.

Different Customer Priorities

Multiple-channel waiting lines provide additional options for handling customers *with* different service priorities. When there is only one server, priorities can be handled only by manipulating the order of customers in the queue. This is a frequent concern in a small hospital emergency room with only one doctor on duty, where the most gravely ill patient must be treated first. Obviously, when there is more than one of these patients at a time, then tough choices have to be made as to which is treated first. That decision is clearly beyond the scope of the level of analysis discussed here.

When more than one server is available, several options are available for managing priority needs. In one aspect, priority defines a class of customers that are handled in the same way as we decide to handle other classes. These approaches will be discussed in more detail in chapter 6—where we will discuss class management.

Different Line Configurations

More servers also allow some creativity in how the line(s) of customers are arranged, particularly when some servers are dedicated to a particular customer class or priority. In addition to improving service performance, important considerations for line configuration design are the psychological effects on customers and opportunities to inform customers as to what they can do to help speed up the service process.

A common example of different line configuration approaches used in many banks, post offices, and airport security check-ins was shown in Figure 3.1. From a strict average performance business viewpoint, both the separate line per server and one line feeding all servers (the "snake") configurations have the same average values for service performance.

The difference between the two configurations is found in individual customer waiting time experiences and psychological impressions. Because of this, the configuration choice is more dependent on managerial attitudes and prior experience rather than actual numbers. We will discuss this topic in more detail in chapter 6 where we will focus on managerial concerns.

Service Capability Variations

In chapter 3 and this chapter, our analysis has assumed a consistent service rate for each server. In reality, we all know that this assumption is often invalid based on our experience in a line where a new teller or checkout clerk is learning on the job. Most service activities are repetitive in nature, and repetition makes a person more proficient (faster and more accurate) as he or she gains experience doing that task. Such improvement is more dramatic at first and slowly diminishes in magnitude over time until the person's performance essentially flattens out to a steady level. Some good examples are learning how to ride a bicycle or memorizing commonly used reference values or coffee recipes instead of having to look them up each time you need them.

Learning curves can be used to estimate the time to reach a given proficiency if there is information available as to what percentage of improvement over time is typical for a given job content. In general, the more repetition and less variety of tasks involved, the faster the improvement rate. The learning curve equation is based on the concept that every time the total number of repetitions of a task is doubled, the amount of time per repetition is reduced by a constant percentage. The equation for a learning curve takes the following form:

$$T_n = T_1 \times n^b \quad \text{where } b = \frac{\ln(\%)}{\ln(2)}. \tag{5.14}$$

Here T_n is the time to do the nth repetition, T_1 is the time to do the first repetition, and the % sign is the learning percentage value. A learning percentage value of 80% (0.8) corresponds to a 20% reduction in time per repetition every time the total number of repetitions doubles. So a higher learning percentage corresponds to a slower improvement in proficiency (100% = no improvement with repetitions).

If you have some data regarding how long each successive repetition takes for your situation, you can estimate your typical learning percentage in two different ways. The first method is more universal but a bit more complicated:

$$\% = 2^{\left(\frac{\ln(T_n/T_1)}{\ln(n)}\right)}. \tag{5.15}$$

The other method is to take the ratio of any pair of repetition times, where the number of repetitions for one time is double or half the number of repetitions for the other time. Then the learning percentage is the shorter time divided by the longer time. That is, the $\% = T_x/T_{x/2}$ or T_{2x}/T_x.

Figure 5.1 shows several learning curves with different learning percentages. A table of the values used for the different learning curve percentages and numbers of repetitions in Figure 5.1 is in appendix C.

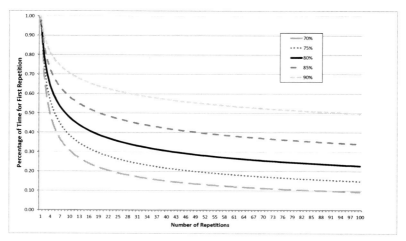

Figure 5.1. Learning curves showing the decrease in time required per repetition as the number of repetitions increase experience for different learning rates. Contrary to intuition, the higher the learning curve percentage, the longer it takes to acquire proficiency.

Example 5.2. Service Time Reduction Learning Rates

How long does it take for a server to become proficient in a given service activity? Searching the Internet can provide some estimates of what others think the time is if there is insufficient information for your business. For example, Grasing (2011) comments that many banking people estimate that it takes typically 3 months for a new teller to reach full proficiency, and a teller typically should be able to handle an average of 30 transactions per hour at that level. Like many pieces of information on the Internet, we must ask, "Are these realistic estimates by the banking crowd?" before proceeding to use them for our analysis. One verification is the article by Kotha et al. (1996), where they relate how the management at KeyCorp initiated a campaign that reduced average service time down from slightly more than 4 minutes to less than 2 minutes. This result is consistent with the value of 30 transactions per hour reported by Grasing.

Let us assume a relatively slow learning curve of 90% and use a T_n of 2 minutes from the 30 transactions per hour expectation. Further, let us assume that it takes about 10 minutes (T_1) for a new teller to do a transaction for the first time. Manipulating Equation 5.14 to solve for n, the number of repetitions required to achieve a proficiency of 30 transactions per hour, we obtain

$$\ln(n) = (1/b) \times \ln(T_n/T_1) \text{ where } b = -0.152 \text{ for a learning percentage}$$
$$\text{of } 90\%.$$

Plugging in the other values, we get $\ln(n) = 10.588191 \rightarrow n = 39,664$. Is this a realistic value? As a check, consider how many transactions could be done in 3 months by a proficient teller at an average of 30 transactions per hour. For thirteen 40-hour workweeks, the total would be 15,600 transactions. We are obviously off here either in the learning percentage, the first task time estimate, or both. Assuming that a typical business would more likely have an accurate estimate of the time required for the first repetition, we will stay with our 10-minute first-repetition time. Hence a faster learning rate estimate is needed to reduce the total number of repetitions required to reach an average 2-minute transaction time. Because of the exponential nature of this learning curve formula, only a small adjustment is required. Using a learning percentage of 88.5%, we obtain -0.176 for b and 9,242 transactions for n. This is a more reasonable result because we would expect that the total number of transactions for a new employee over 3 months would be less than 15,600. It also indicates that the estimate of 3 months by the banking crowd reported by Grasing is more likely a worst-case value.

Is 3 months too long for a service employee to become proficient? Shortening the amount of time required would be to the advantage of any business. It obviously depends on the skills needed and the complexity of the tasks to be done. An earlier edition of a popular college operations management textbook[4] used a bakery to illustrate the use of various manufacturing process strategies in a single business. In the video of the bakery operations that accompanied the text, the bakery manager commented on the typical training time for new employees for each process. The highly automated bread process required only a few weeks, work in a pastry shop required about 3 months, and a cake decorator required about 6 months to become proficient. Because effective training approaches often are dependent on the right managerial support, we will reserve further discussion about such methods for chapter 6.

CHAPTER 6

Managerial Considerations

This chapter covers topics where an astute managerial choice can minimize uncertainties and improve overall performance for businesses affected by some form of waiting line behavior. The areas of consideration include the following:

- Variances in waiting line performance, which includes looking at variances from the customer and the business points of view plus estimating the risks of worst-case scenarios
- Waiting line cost factors
- Cost trade-off analysis
- Service improvement approaches
- Use of customer participation to reduce waiting and service time
- Waiting line configuration considerations
- Psychological factors (While difficult to quantify, these factors are significant considerations that are interlinked with many other areas in this list.)
- Arrival rate management methods
- Options for dealing with priorities, such as more urgent need, rush orders, and preferred customers

Some of you may have jumped ahead to this chapter because you feel that you already know all you have to know about waiting line theory. That may be true for some; but for most, it would be wise to review at least some of the topics in chapters 2 through 5 if parts of the following discussion are confusing.

Variance and Risk Considerations

When I ask business students to select the better business solution after giving them the average performance for each choice, most of them quickly choose the one with the highest average. When more than one choice has the same average performance, the same group often comments that any choice will do.

A few students will look beyond the average performance to considerations of risk or the accuracy of the average performance value before making their choice. To evaluate risk or accuracy, some knowledge of the variances in a process is necessary. Unfortunately waiting line equations provide only steady-state average performance. Start-up variances, such as whether there is a line of customers waiting when a business opens its doors or there is a set of items left over from the previous day of production that need to be completed before beginning new work, are not included in steady-state results. Larger variances, such as no customers or a large group of customers that arrive all at once during the day, occur less often; but when they do, they can cause significant business disruptions.

Risks such as the probability the line will be longer than the capacity of the business can be calculated, but *when* that condition can occur over a period of time cannot be predicted. Managers need to remember that waiting line arrivals and service times are *memoryless.* That is, what happens next is not influenced by what has just happened in the past. For example, when flipping a coin, the next coin toss result is unaffected by whether or not there were two heads, two tails, a head and a tail, or tail and a head for the previous two tosses.

One variance often not considered is the potential variance in normal service and arrival times when waiting lines are much longer or shorter than usual. This is often referred to as a *state-dependent* variance or rate.[1]

When waiting lines get long, some newly arriving customers may be discouraged from entering the line (balking), and some current customers may choose to give up and leave (reneging). At the same time, many servers feel the pressure to speed up their work to help move the line faster. As a result, this creates three general managerial concerns:

1. Arrival rate variances caused by balking or reneging result in lost business opportunities, which was discussed in earlier chapters.

2. When the line is short, a server may unnecessarily chat with a current customer or otherwise work more slowly. This reduces the opportunity for the server to do other work useful for the business.

3. When the line is long, servers may work faster by taking shortcuts and perhaps not being as careful to prevent mistakes, which, when they occur, often offset any time gained because of the time required to correct them. This affects the customer's perception of the service quality received and can be quite serious if the mistake is preparing or assembling the wrong order, omitting something from the order, or making an error in recording the payment and giving the customer change.

Clear managerial communication and good server training can minimize server variances by letting servers know they will not be penalized for remaining careful and not taking shortcuts when lines are long and making clear any requirements regarding what servers are expected to do during times when no customers are present.

In manufacturing lines, some of the arrival rate variances can be minimized through careful production scheduling; but when dealing with customers, we have to work with service rate variances unless the business is conducive to using an appointment or reservation system. In customer service lines, reneging and balking can be reduced by opening up a temporary express window for customers with standard, easy-to-do needs. An advantage of this approach is that you can use a staff person who may not be trained in the full range of services offered. An example of this is opening up a window strictly for customers only picking up mail and/or packages at post offices when the line is long. So, how do we assess potential variances and risks in waiting line performance? We can use three basic steps:

1. Be aware that variances and risks exist and often can be much larger than one would normally expect. In addition, we need to accept that average values predicted by equations are the exception rather than the rule for individual customers or items in a queue. Figure 2.3 illustrates this situation by showing some of the performance data for the first 100 customers entering a typical coffee shop.

2. Collect data about how the business operates. Observing the number of arrivals per period and the number of customers or items in the system at the end of each period allows a determination of waiting times using Little's Law and an estimation of service times. Processing point-of-sale (POS) data can provide estimates of the percentage of different customer classes and service time distributions. So one can develop more accurate discrete distributions for arrival and service rates in simulation models, some of these data collection methods are discussed in more detail in chapter 7.

3. Simulation runs using an accurate model of the given business process can be used to provide more accurate performance values than the queuing models can predict. This is particularly true when the arrival and service distributions for a business are not well described by the basic probability distributions. The simulation runs also can provide a picture over time as to how the performance values can vary and identify the possible worst-case and best-case scenarios. The caveat here is that the simulation results are useful only if the simulation model accurately represents how the particular business actually operates. Some of the chapter 7 simulation examples illustrate how to calculate data regarding possible variances.

Variances that are very difficult to quantify are differences in customer attitudes. Their tolerance of waiting times and long lines can vary greatly depending on the time of day, the weather, whether they are with a friend or not, whether their service need is urgent or not, any personal time limitations, and so forth. Although we cannot usually address the direct causes of these variations, we can reduce their intensity by considering the psychological factors associated with waiting. Some of these factors and methods for reducing their effects are discussed later in this chapter. *The most important consideration to remember when accounting for variability in waiting line business decisions is that the variances experienced by the business are NOT directly related to the variances encountered by customers.*

Waiting Line Costs

Many of us have been in the situation where the cost information is scanty, but our boss requires a quick decision. So, what do we do? We make the best decision we can with what data we have and fill in the gaps with our intuition and past experiences. This is a pretty good solution in many business situations, but when waiting line characteristics are involved, we need to recognize that there is a much higher level of uncertainty because we no longer can count heavily on our intuition and experience to guide us to a reasonable answer.

When evaluating cost trade-offs, you should recognize that such analysis is only as good as the understanding you have regarding your business. Estimated values result in only ballpark guesses as to the best choice. Even worse is when you are unaware of a background activity that is necessary for you to be able to provide your service. Many of the textbook examples for waiting lines focus only on "front-office" activities when evaluating cost. However, some process changes when directly dealing with customers can have a significant effect on "back office" processes. Therefore, it is strongly recommended that you *and* your staff develop a service blueprint[2] of your business to help take into account all the costs and performance factors affecting its outcome.

The simple graph in Figure 1.4 shows the basic idea that the total operational cost of a waiting line has some minimal value per customer served or item produced when the proper balance of resources and customer satisfaction is achieved. Adding more resources and/or improving service performance reduce the waiting time and the length of the queue.

- For manufacturing applications, this correlates to faster throughput time and reduced work-in-process (WIP) inventories.
- For repair and maintenance activities, this means that equipment is not out of service for as long, which reduces the size of the equipment fleet required for adequate service capacity.
- For customer applications, this correlates to retaining more customers, reducing the possibility of balking, and increasing the business volume that be accommodated.

The basic trade-off that must be considered, therefore, is as follows: "If I add more resources to improve service, is there enough reduction in waiting and other costs to more than pay for those resources?"

Table 6.1. Some Cost Components to Be Considered When Seeking a Minimal Cost Balance Between Waiting Costs and Resource Costs

Cost	Symbols	Components	Data Sources
Balking	C_B	Lost customers, bad PR	Marketing
Blocking	C_B	Limited capacity K	M/M/s/K model
Reneging	C_B	Line not moving fast enough	Marketing
Waiting time	C_W	Waiting time in line, total time in service process	All models and simulation
Throughput time	C_W	Waiting time in line, total time in service process, capacity	Simulation
Financing	$C_\$$	Credit interest, insurance	Accounting
Spoilage	$C_\$$	Production loss, step yields, perishable inventory, theft	Accounting and manufacturing
Warehouse space	C_H, C_F	Inventory holding costs, rent	All models and Accounting
Lost business capacity	$C_\$$	Repair time, line length, population size N, late penalties	M/M/s/∞/N model
Appointment delays	$C_\$$	Appointment schedule, service time variation	All models and simulation
Staffing	C_S	Salaries, benefits	Accounting and human resources
Equipment	C_E	Price, maintenance, spare parts, depreciation	Vendor and accounting
Facility	C_F	Construction, permits, rent, maintenance, capacity, security, insurance, utilities, janitorial services	Vendors, accounting, service process

Table 6.1 lists several cost values that are needed to make useful waiting line business decisions. The list is not intended to be inclusive, but it provides enough items to help you identify the types of costs that you should consider for your business decisions. Table 6.1 also gives some symbols that we will use here to simplify the equations for analyzing cost trade-offs. Many textbook authors use C to represent cost, with a subscript or parenthetical notation to represent the particular type of cost. For example,

$$C(Total) = C(Waiting) + C(Service)$$

or

$$C_{Total} = C_{Waiting} + C_{Service}.$$

Here we will use a larger set of cost symbols, which are defined in greater detail in appendix B. This helps us remember that there are several waiting-cost and service-cost components, as indicated in Tables 6.1 and 6.2.

It is rare that you can trade off one waiting cost factor against one resource-cost factor without having some effect on other cost factors. Therefore, do not be surprised if the result of your decision is not exactly what your analysis told you.

Volume-related costs, such as utilities[3] and the materials associated with what each customer or item requires for service, are usually ignored in cost trade-off analyses unless the supplies are perishable (such as food) and the cost decision has a direct effect on the amount of spoilage. Where things get complicated is how we handle floor space costs. If these costs are solely due to business volume (more total customers → more space),

Table 6.2. Some Waiting and Resource Costs to Be Considered When Working With Different Categories of Waiting Line Applications

Typical Application	Waiting Costs: C_B, C_L, C_W, and C_H	Resource Costs: C_S, C_E, and C_F
Coffee shop, bank	Balking, blocking, waiting time, reneging	Staffing, equipment, facility
Single source: passport office, department of motor vehicles, licensing, other government agencies	Waiting time	Staffing, equipment, facility
Manufacturing line	Throughput time, financing, spoilage, warehouse space	Equipment, staffing, facility
Self-service	Reneging, waiting time	Equipment
Repair and maintenance	Lost business (capacity reduction), spare equipment	Staffing, equipment, facility
Call centers	Blocking, reneging, waiting time	Staffing, equipment, hold capacity
Parking lots	Blocking, reneging, waiting time	Facility, maintenance
Health clinics, professional services	Appointment delays	Staffing, facility

then they are usually not a factor in determining the minimal total value. But if more floor space is required to not turn away potential customers, then the profits gained from the increased number of customers per period must exceed the increased facility cost per period.

Lost business capacity and lost profit costs are similar in that both lose a potential profit. Lost business capacity is when you lose some of your normal capacity for a short time, such as when a resource is delayed in the repair shop when you had planned to use that resource to satisfy an existing customer order. Lost profit is when your normal capacity is insufficient to accommodate a customer who would have entered your business to place an order if not discouraged by a long line or insufficient capacity for waiting customers. Lost business capacity often has additional losses because you may have to pay a late-delivery penalty to the customer, or the customer may cancel the order after you have already put some work into its completion.

A tricky cost component is the percentage of server idle time. Most businesses include it as part of the service costs associated with a server. However, when P_0 is more than 10% to 15% of an individual server's time, there is an opportunity to reduce total costs by asking the server to do some routine maintenance or other support tasks instead of assigning them to back-office staff. In businesses with a staff of several servers, this practice could reduce the overall staffing needs by one or more people.

You may notice that I did not specifically list line length in the waiting costs column for Table 6.2. Line length plays a part when considering a limited capacity situation (M/M/1/K and M/M/s/K models), where the length of the line affects blocking costs. However, it is the time spent waiting in line that is the primary cost driver in many situations. The old adage "time is money" applies very well here. To help illustrate why line length is not as important as waiting time, consider Example 6.1. You may feel the background information is more than needed, but the intent is to illustrate the importance of considering factors that, at first glance, may not seem relevant to the goal of reducing total costs.

A special category included in Table 6.2 is when there is only one possible source for the service, such as a government agency (passport office, driver's license bureau, business registration, the courts, airport security, etc.). In such situations, balking, lost customers, and customer satisfaction are not likely costs, and the only issue of primary interest is providing enough capacity in the form of facilities and staff to meet the average demand within some maximum time limit at the lowest cost possible. I have not included post offices in this category because many countries have alternatives to official government agencies for mail and package shipments.

Several examples follow to illustrate approaches for determining cost trade-offs for waiting line situations. Example 6.1 describes some basic cost calculations, and Examples 6.2 and 6.3 illustrate the nature of things to consider for more complex cost trade-off analyses. For a good discussion regarding total cost analysis for queuing situations, readers are referred to the online chapter 26 supplement by Hillier and Lieberman (2010).[4]

Example 6.1. Sandwich Stand Cost Trade-Offs

Samantha runs a small sandwich stand on the streets of Portland, Oregon, selling three types of ready-to-go sandwiches for $3.05 each. Because Oregon does not have a sales tax and her costs per sandwich are $2.80, she nets $0.25 per sandwich. We will also assume here that Samantha has learned her market very well and is careful to not make more sandwiches than she can sell in a day. When business is brisk, Samantha sells out more quickly and gets a longer afternoon off. For the few times she has any sandwiches left, Samantha cheerfully donates them to the local homeless shelter at the end of the day. Thus we will not consider monetary losses due to surplus sandwiches that must be discarded.

Samantha has been studying waiting line theory when she gets off early and has decided to collect some data about her business and see if it really works. She determines that it takes about 1 minute for a customer to choose which type of sandwich and pay for it. By checking the reduction in her inventory during her peak hours, she also has determined that the average number of customers between 11:30 a.m. and 1:30 p.m. is 54 per hour.

Using these values for λ and μ, Samantha determined that the utilization factor during the peak period is 0.9, the average line length (L) should be 9 customers, and the average total time for a customer to get a sandwich is 10 minutes. Because the author of her waiting line book has stressed that average values are rarely actually experienced by customers, she concluded that if some customers get their sandwiches in less than 10 minutes, then others have to wait longer than that. Thinking further, Samantha realized that because lunch-time customers do not want to spend any more time than necessary to get their lunches, she is likely losing some customers to other food vendors when her line gets longer.

Wishing to reduce the average waiting time, Samantha worked on the only factor within her control—service time. Observing transactions for several days, Samantha noticed that the major part of the service time was making change for customers, particularly dealing with coins. In the interest of learning more about waiting line theory, Samantha decided to invest some of her profit in an experiment to shorten service time by reducing the price to $3.00, eliminating the need for handling coins. After a week, Samantha observed that this change reduced the average service time by 10 seconds, increasing her average service rate per hour from 60 to 72.

Plugging her new average service time into the M/M/1 equations, Samantha now determined that L should be 3 customers—a dramatic improvement from 9 customers. But she was puzzled because such a change should have been evident, yet she had not noticed significant line differences during the lunchtime period. She was also selling out her stock of sandwiches earlier in the day, which agreed with the faster service time. What could be wrong with her analysis? Then she remembered to recheck her sales rate during the peak time and discovered that it had increased from 54 to 65 customers per hour. Plugging that value into the M/M/1 equations resulted in a revised average line length of 9 customers and an average total time in line of 8.57 minutes per customer. The line length did not change, but the average time in the system did.

At this point, let us step back and look at what happened here. First, line lengths can stay the same while total waiting time changes as long as the utilization factor remains the same. That is, service rates keep up with increased arrival rates. Stated another way, arrival rates tend to increase when service times are reduced because customers can get faster service. The length of a line is not as important to customers if they perceive the line is moving faster (a psychological factor to consider). In this case, Samantha's stand attracted more customers because they could observe the line moving more quickly (the price reduction and customers not having to deal with coinage could also be contributors). (Note: I fudged the amount of the service time reduction to illustrate more clearly that the same line length could have different waiting times.)

Let us look at the profit margin during the peak period for the two scenarios: 108 × $0.25 versus 130 × $0.20 → $27 versus $26. From a profit viewpoint, the process improvement cost Samantha $1.00 of profit based on the lunchtime results, but we should take into account the effect of the improved service time on Samantha's business the rest of the day and the possibility for her to sell more sandwiches per day before deciding whether or not to continue offering the sandwiches for $3.00.

Given the nature of Samantha's service process, there are limited possibilities for her to reduce her service time. In such cases, the primary option is to add another server at the peak time. Referring to the table in appendix C and using Samantha's initial value of $\rho = 0.9$, adding one more server would reduce the average line length to 1.1285 customers, and the average total time to get a sandwich would decrease to 1.25 minutes. Now Samantha has an estimate of how many more customers she can expect to attract by reducing waiting time from her service time reduction experiment, so she estimated that with the even better performance provided by another server, she could keep the increased volume and also charge her original price of $3.05. Would this pay for the cost of another server? Running the numbers, the increased profit would be $5.50—not enough to pay minimum wage for even an hour.

The conclusion here is that sometimes the options available for improving a particular service process are not enough for the customer volume and profit model associated with that process. In Samantha's case, she would have to have significantly higher volume to justify hiring another server. Just shortening the waiting time and the average line length are not likely to attract that many more customers; other things such as expanding her sandwich choices, adding beverages to the selection, and so forth, would be needed, which, in turn, would introduce a whole new set of cost factors.

To illustrate situations where reasonable service improvements could pay off in lower total cost, we will discuss three more examples. The first is a classic repair service problem, where long turnaround times could cost a company significant money. The second is a manufacturing system where WIP inventory is expensive. The third is evaluating the benefit of adding more space to accommodate longer lines. Working through the solutions is left to the reader as an exercise; each example discusses the situation, indicates what costs should be considered, and how one might go about determining the best solution.

Example 6.2. Helicopter Shuttle Business Costs
This business provides regular flights for residents of a small rural city to the nearest major airport located some distance away. The business goals are to not miss a regularly scheduled departure—because being late could cause greater hardship for their passengers—and accomplish that performance at a minimum total cost. Operational cost factors to consider include keeping the size of the helicopter as small as possible because helicopters are costly to own and maintain, determining the number of daily flights required to satisfy customer demand, the routine maintenance schedule required by the Federal Aviation Administration, how many reserve helicopters are required, the likelihood of unexpected breakdowns, and the possibility of unavailable staff due to illness or vacation. Some factors to compare are the costs of having or leasing spare helicopters versus reducing the average maintenance time by either adding staff to existing service crews to reduce the average service time, adding one or more service crews plus the facilities to support them to reduce maintenance and repair waiting time, or paying for some on-call staff. Performance and total costs for each business option can be evaluated using the $M/M/s/\infty/N$ model, where s, N, and μ and their unit costs are the variables.

For some specific examples discussed in detail, Hillier and Leiberman (2010), chapter 17, section 17.10, is a good place to start.

Example 6.3. Factory Inventory Costs
A small business runs a factory line customizing an expensive large product with just one operation step. The demand for this product does not allow using a production schedule to help manage the average line length; thus its arrival rate is best described by an exponential distribution. The inventory costs associated with the average line length can be quite high for this product. Some factors to compare, with the goal of achieving the lowest total cost, are inventory financing costs (price and interest) and warehouse costs (facility space, rent, handling, security, utilities, and insurance) versus hiring more staff to reduce waiting time or buying new or additional equipment to reduce service time. Performance and total costs for each business option can be evaluated using the M/M/s model, where s and μ and their unit costs are the variables.

Example 6.4. Ice Cream Shop with Limited Customer Space
A small ice cream shop occasionally loses customers on hot summer days because it can only accommodate a small number of customers within the store. Is it worth adding more space for the line to accommodate more customers? The factors to compare are the lost profit per customer not accommodated versus adding floor space, reducing the average line length (which reduces the probability that the line will exceed the current available space) by adding staff, or reducing the average service time by buying equipment or otherwise improving the service. Costs can be evaluated for all possible business options using the M/M/s/K model.

Improving Service Performance

There are several basic goals to consider when improving service performance. Some of these are strictly from the business perspective—reducing total cost, completing services faster, and accommodating higher customer volume. Others are from the customer perspective—not having to wait as long for service, a lower service charge, perceived fairness, and a more pleasant waiting experience. Because some of the possible approaches apply to both perspectives, they are listed first.

- Reducing the variation in service times reduces the average waiting time, even if the average service time remains the same (see chapter 4).
- Reduce the average service time.
- Reduce the average waiting time.
- Add capacity—more servers, more waiting space.

Variation reduction is normally the least expensive approach because you are working on using existing resources more effectively. Standardizing all or part of the services provided reduces the variation in service time and reduces the average waiting time, even when the average service time remains the same. In Example 6.1, Samantha standardized part of her service by having sandwiches ready-to-go rather than assembling them to order. This reduced both variability and the duration of the average service time, allowing a single server, Samantha, to handle more customers. She could provide more selections without adding to the service time by setting up a condiment station so that customers can add their own condiments rather than asking her to do it, which would increase her average service time and also add more variability to that time.

Of course, Samantha will have to spend some time to maintain the condiment station, but this can be done during any idle time when there are no customers. For her utilization factor of 0.9, $P_0 = 10\%$, which gives her an average of 6 minutes per hour to maintain the station. The hidden cost factors to be considered are Samantha's choice of method for obtaining ready-to-go sandwiches—typically a classic make versus buy decision.

Another approach for reducing service time variability is to replace the manual parts of a service with more automated methods. This in effect is another form of standardization most often applied to manufacturing situations, but it can also be used effectively in service situations. For example, consider the coffee machines at many gasoline station convenience stores. The cost trade-off considered here is whether having a person keep a hot pot of coffee ready to pour a cup when a customer wants it or having a machine prepare the coffee for the customer on demand is the least expensive option. Doing the cost comparison involves not only the difference and variability in average service times between the two options but also the consideration of spoilage with the manual method, variation in the coffee preparation time, equipment and maintenance costs for either option, and response times for a sudden jump in customer volume (probability the coffee pot is empty, the time to brew a full pot versus the fixed response time for a machine).

Reducing the average service time reduces the average waiting time while increasing the capacity of the service system. Adding more servers is often the first strategy employed to reduce the average service time. But this also increases the probability of no customers in the system (idle time). Normally, the cost of adding servers is offset in the cost analysis by reductions in waiting-time costs and expected increases in customer volume. Hidden cost factors that are not often considered are the possibility of using idle server time to do other tasks required by the business that are not directly related to serving customers. Some examples are managing inventory and cleaning and restocking equipment or service areas, such as a convenience store coffee machine or Samantha's condiment station. This, of course, requires servers who have more flexible job skills and thus may require a higher salary. The primary focus here should be that the added staff is hired primarily to be a server.

The opposite approach is when a staff member hired primarily for a back-office activity is asked to serve customers during periods of peak demand. The limitation of course is that such staff is often not very skilled in performing the full range of service activities, but they can be used for providing simpler, more standardized services during peak demand periods. This often works well for situations such as banks, post offices, and grocery stores where the customer arrival rates are highly variable during the day.

Reducing the average service time by eliminating unnecessary (non–value-added) steps is a common approach discussed in process management texts, but it can be difficult to do when there is little standardization in the service process. What can be done is to eliminate the execution of some steps by the server and have the customer do them instead. Some examples are having customers fill out forms (health insurance, food orders, address labels, etc.) while they wait instead of the server asking questions and filling out the form for the customer. There is also a psychological benefit in doing this, which will be discussed in more detail later in this chapter.

Another way to reduce the average service time without adding servers is to inform customers about what is expected from them when they reach the server. In fast-food restaurants and coffee shops, displaying the menu with prices in clear view of the line helps reduce the time customers spend at the server window deciding what they want to order. Promptly displaying the amount of payment due after receiving the order reduces more service time by allowing a customer to decide on the payment method or collect the appropriate change while the server either processes the order or forwards it on to the kitchen or the barista. This leads to one of my big rules regarding customer-server interactions: *Uninformed customers require more service time. Use the time spent waiting in line to educate them.*

The current best example of this is the airport security check-in process. Clear and properly located information signs[5] can prepare the customer as to what the customer must do at each step instead of servers having to take time to explain individually what is expected of each customer at each stage of the check-in process. This saves the server's voice and lowers frustration on both the part of the server and the customer.

Reducing the average waiting time is very difficult to do unilaterally because it is so strongly related to the arrival rate and service rates. But it can be reduced for some customers in the arrival population by either separating them into different service classes with different average service times or by assigning them a higher priority. Some common examples of this are as follows:

- Express lines at grocery stores for customers with only a few items
- Windows dedicated for mail pickup at the post office
- Bank tellers dedicated to commercial business customers
- Frequent-traveler express lines at airports, car rental agencies, and hotel check-ins
- Separate coffee shop line for customers just wanting a standard cup of house coffee
- Self-service stations or checkout lines for standardized services
- Moving airline travelers who would otherwise miss their flight to the head of the airline counter check-in lines
- Taking care of more seriously ill patients in an emergency room first

The disadvantage with methods that reduce the average service time and/or the average waiting time for some of your customers by serving them according to priority or class is that if you retain the same resource level with the same total average population, your average service rate will remain the same, but the variability in the waiting time experienced by your customers will increase: Some will have a shorter average waiting time, and others will have a *longer* average waiting time. The old adage "there is no such thing as a free lunch" holds true in waiting line operations.

The "classes" approach requires a multiple-server situation with at least two servers—more if there are several classes to be served separately. Thus, if you do not already have multiple servers, you are in effect adding resources to reduce waiting time. The "priority" approach can be used in both single-channel and multiple-channel waiting line models.

In the classes and priority approaches, the overall average through-put rate remains unchanged provided that in multiple-server applications a server who is normally assigned to higher priority or a specific class of customers is expected to take care of lower priority or other classes of customers when that server is idle (jockeying is allowed in that case). Therefore, from a business viewpoint, capacity and average throughput rate remain unchanged. From the customer viewpoint, some of them are served faster at the expense of other customers now having to wait longer.

At this point, some of you are likely thinking, "Why bother doing this? It sounds like a no-gain situation that rewards only some custom-ers." The answer is that sometimes there is little choice to not do it. For a hospital emergency room, it should be clear that having a priority approach is necessary. Rewarding customers who individually contrib-ute a higher percentage of your profits is a standard business practice to encourage them to continue being your customers when competing with other businesses that also provide such incentives.

What are not so obvious are the potential cost advantages. To keep the mathematics manageable, the basic closed-form, waiting line equa-tions assume that all servers are equally capable of providing the same service rate. In chapter 5, we discussed the situation of how long it would take for a new bank teller to achieve that proficiency. Now consider the advantage of a classes approach that would allow new tellers to handle simple transactions, such as deposits and withdrawals, at first and move to more complicated banking transactions later. Their learning curve would then be broken into two or more learning curves with faster learning percentages.

This leads to an important conclusion: Classes allow the use of a range of server skills, which, in turn, allows the possibility of a range of server costs. For example, consider a three-server application where all the servers are expected to be able to handle the full range of expected customer transactions. But in many situations, part of the normal customer population wants only services that could be done using a self-service machine. Automatic teller machines, online banking, Web check-in, flat-rate package mailing, and convenience store coffee machines are some examples that this is true.

This is where managers earn their salaries. We can do the cost comparisons using the three-server example versus two servers and a machine or even one server versus one or two machines. We can account for the differences in capabilities (flexibility of the server or server substitute) and relative costs, assuming we have a good estimate of how many customers in each class we plan to serve. This is the easier part. What is more difficult is considering the risks involved.

In this situation, if one server becomes ill, it is likely that the service can still be provided but with commensurate longer waiting times. This is also the case when we replace one server with a self-service machine: If the machine breaks down, the two remaining full-service servers can temporarily take up the slack. (In both cases, λ/μ must be less than two for this to be possible.) But if one of the two remaining servers becomes ill, the machine cannot take up the entire sick server's load because of its more limited capability. That is, a server can take all the work of a broken machine, but a machine can take over for only part of a server's work. The risk imposed by this lack of interchangeability increases when cost comparisons indicate to a manager that the most economical situation is two machines and one server.

Considering that more complex transactions are usually more critical, I would want to be sure that they are covered. Therefore, without even looking at the cost comparisons beforehand, I would restrict my cost comparisons for this situation to the three-server or the two-server-plus-machine options.

If some of the possible classes turn out to be a very low percentage of the total population, it is usually better that they be included as part of a larger class. But, if a class is a significant percentage of a business's clientele, it is usually worthwhile to consider how you can provide a separate service or priority for them.

One great example of how to serve one class of customer without adding either servers or machines was at a local coffee shop in Oregon where the owner set up a self-serve station for his customers who just wanted a cup of house coffee. He also eliminated the need for a server to handle payments for the house coffees by posting the price for each size of cup and trusting his customers to put the appropriate amount into a locked cashbox with a slit in it. I observed that almost no customers skipped the payment, and some put in more than what was asked because they did not have adequate change. In this case, he reduced not only the average waiting time for his house coffee customers but also the need for server time to support that part of his business.

So how does a business owner identify such classes of customers? In sales operations, POS data can really help. Some examples are as follows:

- You can screen your POS receipts for the percentage of customers who buy less than a given number of items to determine whether or not an express checkout line would be useful.
- You can screen the POS data for how many customers order products or services that require only a standard service time.
- You can analyze your sales data for your highest volume buyers or service requests.

You can also ask your customers to help by allowing them to select the class of service they want. This is particularly useful for call center and repair service operations. When calling in for support, we all have encountered choice menus that let us identify what type of question we want answered. This not only directs us to the right person to answer that question but also provides data that the call center can use to adjust staffing levels, allows the looking up records by the computer for some requests like asking for your current account balance, or makes the records already available for an operator to reduce the average service time and required staffing levels.

The useful thing is to recognize that when arrival rates are described by exponential distributions with appropriate average values, one can easily combine or separate average arrival rate distributions for the classes. The results will also be exponential distributions with the same general characteristics.

For example, consider a typical banking call center operation where there are three choices (effectively classes where the customer tells you what class they are in) on the telephone menu, such as the following:

1. Account balance check
2. Billing and payment questions
3. All other questions

Assume that the bank knows the average arrival rate for each choice by analyzing its previous call history. We will designate these rates as λ_1, λ_2, and λ_3. Hence the total arrival rate λ to be handled by the call center if it is operated as a multiple-channel, single-phase system where any operator can answer the next call is merely the sum of λ_1, λ_2, and λ_3. Of course, in a large call center with several operators with different skill levels, each individual arrival rate is likely to be assigned to a specific operator or even an automated response for some choice.

Consider a similar situation with the same choices, where the business knows the overall average arrival rate λ for its customer base but has not yet collected enough data to break down that rate into the individual rates for each choice. Wanting to improve its service by possibly designating specific operator(s) or automated responses to each choice, the business checks with a call center consulting firm for information about industry average percentages for each class of questions. The consulting firm provides the values of P_1, P_2, and P_3, respectively, for the business's choices. Because exponential distributions can also be easily separated into components that are also exponential distributions, the bank can then obtain λ_i by multiplying λ by the respective probability P_i.

You can get useful information even when a consulting firm does not have all the usual percentages. This is often the case because your customer base does not match up well with any of the databases that consulting firms might have. Software can monitor the frequency of choices selected in the telephone menu: Given that information, a manager can then decide whether or not to address the choices separately or as a combined pool.

Finally, when improving service performance by adding more servers, the training time required for a new server to achieve an acceptable proficiency level becomes a business priority. Those businesses that can do it faster than their competitors have a competitive edge when the demand for their type of services is increasing.

One common method to increase the learning rate is using a mentor alongside a new employee for the first week or so. It is important that the mentor have the new employee do all the repetitions for the best result. This means that the mentor needs to resist the temptation to step in and do some of the steps for the employee to serve a long line of waiting customers more quickly. In such situations, it is better, if possible, to open up another line to take some of the pressure off the new employee's learning experience.

Another method for businesses that handle different classes of customers separately is to start the new employee with the simpler service operations and then include more complex services as that employee's proficiency increases.

A common example illustrated in Figure 6.1 is the practice of many coffee shops of having one or two servers take customer orders and collect payments and a separate group of baristas prepare the different types of coffees requested. In most instances, the order takers also handle non-preparation services, such as pouring house coffees and taking care of pastry orders. This not only provides a training path but also allows the more effective use of the more highly trained barista staff and the ability to use part-time workers for the order taking. In effect, two lines and two classes have been created here: one for all customers and a second line (phase) for customers with more complex orders.

The most important element is clear communication between the manager and the service employees about the training process and what is expected. This should include how to deal with long-line situations to avoid the state-dependent rate variances discussed earlier.

Waiting Line Configurations, Psychological Factors

Many times, it is not practical or even possible to do much to reduce the average waiting time for a service. First, it is important to not do things that would increase a customer's perception of how long the wait is

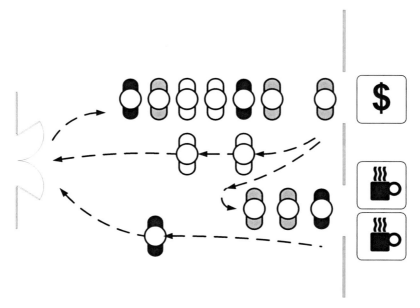

Figure 6.1. Coffee shop waiting line configuration for customers with simple orders (white symbols) and more complex orders (gray and black symbols).

likely to be. Second, there are things we can do to reduce anxiety in line or even to allow a customer to make more effective use of that waiting time. Some suggestions paraphrased from the available online literature are given here; for more detailed information, consult the classic article by Maister (1985) and the following expanded discussion based on Norman (2008).

Some general axioms regarding the waiting experience are as follows:

- If a customer has time limitations, anxiety increases, and the wait appears to be longer. This is especially appropriate for lunchtime customers.
- The more desirable the service, the longer people are willing to wait. Popular restaurants, popular movies and shows, and limited attendance venues are good examples. A corollary here is that excellent service can compensate for some poor waiting conditions.
- The more necessary the service, the more customers will tolerate a long wait.

- Waiting on hold seems longer than waiting in line.
- When there is more than one line, your line always appears to be more slowly. You notice it when the other line moves with respect to you but not when your line moves with respect to the other line.
- Time moves more slowly when you have nothing to do but wait. The corollary is that the wait appears to end more quickly when you have something to do.

Some negative psychological factors to be avoided are as follows:

- A clock on the wall reminds customers of the passage of time.
- Not informing customers about what is to be expected (priority rules, what is required of the customer to obtain service, how long the current average wait is, etc.). One common failure in this regard is the practice of many restaurants to assign specific tables to each server on duty. Customers who are unaware of this can be quite upset when they have been waiting and a nearby server who is not assigned to their table seems to be ignoring them. Some customer dissatisfaction can be avoided by the host or hostess seating customers at their table and telling them who their assigned server will be and perhaps even taking their drink orders to get things started.
- An uncomfortable waiting environment: Expecting people to wait outside in a predominantly rainy climate like the Pacific Northwest or asking medical patients to stand instead of sit while waiting are just cruel practices. When people have other more comfortable waiting options for the service they want, such practices will cost a business many of its customers.

Some positive things a business can do are as follows:

- Give customers something to do while they wait. The best items are things that contribute to completing the service process, such as filling out forms, informing customers about what they will need to do when they reach the server, or letting them know about any personal data or items that may be required for service rather than finding out when they reach the server window after a long wait. In some cases, it is possible to allow a customer to leave the service facility to do other things during the waiting time and then return shortly before they are next in line for service.[6,7]

• Use a single-line configuration for multiple-server applications wherever possible. The single-line and parallel-line configurations in Figure 3.1 provide the same average waiting time from a business perspective, but the variability in individual customer experience and the perception of how fast the line moves are different. The single-line configuration moves every time a single customer is processed; parallel lines move only when a customer in that line is processed. The more servers, the faster the single line moves in respect to individual lines. In addition, the variability in individual customer waiting times is reduced because the effect of individual service times that are very long or very short are averaged out over the number of servers rather than affecting just the line in front of one server.

• Make the waiting area more comfortable and even productive for customers while they wait. Seating, wireless access to the Internet, and self-serve coffee stations have become more common in many waiting areas as businesses become aware that customers who have something to do are more tolerant of uncertain or longer waits.

Arrival Rate Management Methods

Another approach for reducing variability in service processes is to try to control the arrival rate to some degree. The most familiar method is using appointments or reservations. Appointments are used where there is more predictability in the nature of the services requested and the facility capacity and choice of servers are relatively constant. When the service time has a greater range of variability, such as serving meals in a popular restaurant, and a wider choice of servers can serve a given customer, reservations are more appropriate. Other significant factors here are the cost and availability of servers. The higher the skill requirements, the higher the cost per server and the lower the part-time availability is for such skilled individuals—hence the prevalent use of appointments for most professional services.

Consider a typical medical clinic appointment schedule. The facility has a fixed number of medical staff and examination rooms. The capacity of the facility is dependent on the effectiveness of the appointment schedule. Some medical services, such as vaccinations and routine tests, have a relatively constant service time, making their appointment schedule easy if the demand requires it (some daily peaks greater than the daily capacity). The appointment time then becomes whatever the service time is plus some easily calculated small addition to accommodate cleanup and preparation between patients.

But when we consider the appointment schedule for doctors on the staff, life just became more complicated. The factors to be considered are that not all doctors require the same average examination time, examination times can vary considerably from one patient to the next, patients sometimes arrive a bit late, some room must be left in the appointment schedule to accommodate unscheduled urgent care patients,[8] and, most important of all, when a patient examination lasts longer than the allotted appointment time, it affects the timing of some if not all the subsequent appointments that day. Taking all this into account, the goal of an appointment scheduling time analysis is to select an appointment duration that reduces the possibility of an appointment running late without trading off too much patient capacity. The trade-off is between the costs of having people stay later to accommodate the patient who made the last appointment versus accommodating fewer patients during the day.

Having a probability distribution that accurately represents the distribution of examination times is essential. Unfortunately, the standard use of an exponential service distribution to represent service time in general queuing analysis models does not work well here because it allows a high percentage of service times lower than the average time. A normal distribution is more representative of medical examinations, and Erlang or beta distributions are better, but the best is when the clinic has enough data to determine its own discrete distribution for use in simulation programs for scheduling. Example 6.5 illustrates how a normal service time probability distribution can be used to estimate the probability of an appointment running over.

Example 6.5. Appointment Schedule Analysis

A doctor and a nurse are reviewing their appointment schedule to see if they can revise the average appointment time. The goal is reduce the number of evenings working late to take care of the last patient when some appointments run over. Their data shows that the average examination time for a patient takes 15 minutes. They also need an average of 2 minutes to prepare the examination room for the next patient and enter the current patient's medical records into the computer. Their current appointment time is 20 minutes, which allows them to take care of 24 appointment or urgent-care patients in an 8-hour day. They felt that amount of time would provide enough spare time to accommodate an occasional appointment overrun, but experience indicates that it is not enough. They have not accumulated enough data to have an accurate estimate of the variability of the examination times, but they do remember that a few examinations took as long as 30 minutes.[9]

Let's use a normal distribution to see if we can get a rough estimate on what might be a better appointment time. We will use 15 minutes for the mean time and 30 minutes as a worst-case time; then we will estimate the standard deviation σ as being one third of the difference between the maximum time and the mean time, which is 5 minutes. We are assuming here that a $\pm 3\sigma$ distribution around the average time will include almost all (99.74%) of the possible examination times. I have not included the 2 minutes for preparation and record-keeping because this is under the control of the doctor and nurse, does not vary much from patient to patient, and can be made up in different ways that do not affect patient times.

The current overrun margin is $20 - 15 = 5$ minutes or 1σ. Consulting a normal distribution table, the percentage of the normal distribution less than or equal to 20 minutes is 84.13%, so there is a 15.87% chance that an examination will take longer than 20 minutes. Because there are currently 24 appointment periods per day, an average of $0.1587 \times 24 = 3.8$ appointments will run over each day. This, of course, does not tell us when those overrun appointments will occur during the day. If they all occur early in the day, almost all patients will have to wait longer for their appointments. If they all occur late in the day, the doctor and nurse will really be working late. Thus, when the overruns occur is very important for this analysis.

If the doctor and nurse increase the appointment time to 25 minutes, the probability of an overrun drops to 2.28%, which is less than one appointment overrun per day. But we also have reduced the number of appointments per day from 24 to 19, a capacity loss of 20.8%. This would create a need to add facilities and doctors somewhere else to take care of the 5 patients who are being turned away.

Example 6.5 is a simplified problem that illustrates the need for using simulation methods, where the effect of various appointment times and different overrun times can be evaluated to determine the best result that provides the highest capacity without undue costs and customer waits. A normal distribution is rarely the best distribution for scheduling purposes, but it is often used because it is easier to use in queuing analysis models and more familiar to many users.

Some other observations are that if the examination room preparation and patient record entry could be handled independently of the doctor and the nurse, it would free up another 2 minutes per appointment. For example, you could have a dedicated record clerk do the entries and a dedicated attendant prepare examination rooms.

Staggering the appointment times so that each doctor in a practice does not start appointments at the same times would simplify the scheduling of these back-office support activities. Staggering appointment times would also space out appointment check-ins for a smoother process flow at the check-in desk and provide a positive psychological effect in the waiting room because patients would be arriving and departing on a more regular basis, not intermittently in groups.

Actual operational data are necessary to provide the best representations of the service time and arrival time distributions in simulations. It cannot be emphasized enough that the result of a simulation is only as good as the knowledge of the real-life process and the actual operational data available for it.

For this medical clinic problem, the following data are needed for an accurate simulation solution:

- A history of actual examination times is needed to build an accurate discrete probability distribution for those times.
- A history of appointment overruns, how long each was, and what time of day it occurred gives a picture of the typical overrun.
- Separate this information into values associated with regular patients and values associated with unscheduled urgent-care patients. (It is likely that longer examination times are more closely associated with urgent-care patients, but this assumption should be verified.)
- Identify the number of urgent-care patients per day per class of care. This helps in planning the number of open appointments needed per day and how they might be shared among the doctors who are most capable of handling the particular class of care required.[10]
- Identify the history of times that patients arrived for an appointment: how early or late were they and what time of day was the appointment. Such arrival timing variations can contribute to overruns and hinder the ability to catch up after an overrun or even get ahead of schedule.

Reservation policies have similar constraints and data collection needs, but they allow some simplifications because the number of reservations required per day is more limited. For many popular restaurants, the number of successive reservations (turns) for a given location is limited to how many groups they expect to seat at that location during a normal dining period (breakfast, lunch, or dinner). Obviously, the restaurant will require an estimate of how long customers will typically take to order and eat their meals and also must recognize that their service rate contributes to this period. One rule of thumb to help judge the variability of dining time is that the larger the group, the longer one might expect customers will take for dinner because of the increased amount of socializing (and beverages) that are likely to occur.

In many European restaurants, a group has the table for the evening, so the likelihood of a late-night reservation is not considered. In that respect, such restaurants are no different from one-time events, such as airplane flights, hotel rooms, Broadway shows, and sporting events. The challenge here is to fill the available seats or rooms for maximum profit. There is always some risk that someone with a reservation will cancel at the last minute. Knowing the average number of no-shows based on their past experience, some businesses will accept that number of reservations over their available capacity to ensure full usage of that capacity. The risk they take on is possibly having to deal with a highly dissatisfied customer who has a reservation and no accommodation because the usual number of no-shows did not occur. This practice, called overbooking, is used by many airlines and hotels. While overbooking analysis also involves working with arrival distributions and probabilities, it is not included in the scope of this monograph.[11]

Priority Management

To conclude this chapter, some discussion regarding suggested guidelines for using priorities in waiting line applications is in order. We will cover this in two parts: people and items. When dealing with people, one basic rule to remember is that when you selectively improve the waiting experience of one group in a queue, you have also chosen to make that experience worse for the other groups in the queue. Another basic rule to also consider is that when dealing with systems *where all servers are equally capable of handling all customers,* priority management does not affect the overall average performance.

Simply put, moving some people to the head of the line makes others wait longer. If you do this too often in a single line, you run the risk of delaying some customers long enough that they give up and leave the line without being served. If the reason you give some customers priority is not explained or appears to be unfair to the remaining customers, you risk losing even more customers who will take their business elsewhere.

Dealing with these issues is easy in some situations. Giving preference to more critically ill patients in an emergency room is generally understood by the other patients and even expected. Another commonly understood preference is when passengers who would otherwise miss their flights are called to the head of the line at the airline ticket counter. The announcement not only helps identify who needs preference but also tells the others why they are being given preference.

Giving preference to more valuable customers on hold in a call center is easy because the process is invisible to other customers on hold and the selection can even be automated. For face-to-face professional services, some businesses even use separate entrances for preferred customers to achieve a form of call center anonymity.

When the number of customers requiring some preference is relatively large, it is better to treat them as a class and set up either a separate line (frequent travelers at an airport) or a business process like an express line at a grocery store to handle them. This also helps communicate to other customers the reason for the different treatment to reduce their impressions of being treated unfairly.

Nonpreemptive and Preemptive Priorities

There are two ways to handle higher-priority customers: nonpreemptively and preemptively.

A nonpreemptive approach moves a higher-priority customer to the head of the waiting line, allowing a lower-priority customer currently being served to continue being served until that service is completed. A preemptive approach allows a higher-priority customer (A) to replace a lower-priority customer (B) currently being served, delaying the completion of the service for B until later when there are no more higher-priority customers to preempt B. If there are a large number of higher-priority customers, B is likely to wait a long time before his or her service can be completed.

The nonpreemptive approach is preferred for most call center priority applications because it best preserves the invisibility aspect of the prioritization process. (Imagine being asked to be put back on hold while the operator takes care of another caller.) It is also preferred in most applications where immediate service is not the sole reason for the priority and where the line behavior is observable by all customers because it is perceived as being fairer than the preemptive approach.

While this should be intuitively obvious, using priorities increases the variability of waiting times: the higher the percentage of customers getting preferential treatment, the higher the variability. Because variability adds uncertainty to business outcomes, using priority rules in processing waiting line customers should be carefully considered; if used, it should be limited to only a small percentage of the arrival population.

Some models[12,13] have been developed to determine the increased variability in average waiting time when using both nonpreemptive and preemptive priorities. These models also aid in determining the degree of reduction in the average waiting time for higher-priority customers and the concomitant increase in waiting time for lower-priority customers. If you are interested in possibly applying these models to your situation, consult Hillier and Lieberman (2010), chapter 17, and Haussmann (1970). Be sure to review the assumptions and conditions for using such models to make sure they are appropriate for your situation.

An effective use of intermittent preemptive prioritization is when a customer being served needs to fill out a form or otherwise do something that only the customer can do to complete the service. Instead of asking the customers waiting in line to wait longer while this is done by the customer, the server asks the customer to leave the line to fill out the form or do the other activity and then reenter the head of the line when done, in effect giving that customer a higher priority. Such a line is occasionally referred to as a double-ended queue or dequeue. This has several benefits with no additional cost to the business to implement it; it reduces the average service and waiting times, improves customer satisfaction, and is generally viewed by customers as a fair use of prioritization.[14]

Manufacturing applications can use a wider range of priority rules when dealing with items or jobs with varying service times. These rules are normally applied as part of the production scheduling process. At the beginning of each day, the production scheduler reviews the list of jobs or items to be produced and then sequences them according to the priority rule used. Some of the more commonly used rules[15,16] are as follows: shortest process time first (SPT), first-come, first-served (FCFS) or first-in, first-out (FIFO), earliest due date (EDD), slack per remaining operation (S/O or SRO), critical ratio (CR), and Johnson's Rule (for the special case of two sequential steps with varying service times at each).

Performance measures for such schedules include the average number of jobs or work-in process (WIP inventory—same as L in queuing analysis), the average job lateness (missing any due dates), the job flow time (same as W in queuing analysis), and makespan (the total time to complete a group of jobs).[17]

It should be obvious that the scheduling goal is to minimize the value for each measure. Because priority rules do not all affect performance measures to the same degree or in the same manner, a manager should select a rule that best addresses the performance measure that is most important for that manager's business. If all jobs must go through the same sequence of steps or operations, the queuing analysis models discussed in this monograph can be used to determine which scheduling priority rule provides the lowest performance measure values for a particular business.

However, when the job flow is not the same for all items, which occurs in many job shops, most queuing models are inadequate for the task. There is considerable work in progress to develop good mathematical models for job shop situations, but the mathematics involved is challenging, and the current results available are usually difficult to understand by someone who does not have strong mathematical or statistical skills.

One special priority rule used in manufacturing is the practice of using "hot lots" for preferentially moving selected items or jobs through a process faster. While in practice it is best to avoid the need for expediting items through a manufacturing process, sometimes it is necessary to satisfy the need of a critical customer or cope with output constraints imposed by a manufacturing process. This need was prevalent in many early integrated circuit fab facilities because of the large variance in final product yields and long manufacturing times of several weeks or more. A problem frequently encountered then with hot lots was that there were often so many rush requests from different customer groups that the reduced processing time advantage for hot lots was so small that it was not worthwhile. This forced many fab managers to put restrictions on the number of hot lots they would accept at any one time. This limit was typically between 5% and 10% based on the experience of a given fab manager. Analysis using one of the priority models available today would have allowed managers to set more appropriate hot-lot limits for a desired expedited throughput time.

In summary, my experience has indicated that using priority systems in queuing applications is less effective when dealing with people and should be generally avoided unless there is a clear justification for them (emergency rooms, 911 calls, etc.). Separating customers into different service classes is a better way to offer improved services to customers.

CHAPTER 7

Useful Tools and Simulation Methods

This chapter discusses some tools that can simplify waiting line analyses and the basic simulation approaches for evaluating variances in waiting line behavior and analyzing situations for which no closed-form mathematical solution yet exists. Specific topics include the following:

- Little's Law
- Waiting line data collection
- Probability distribution determination
- Simulation models
  - o Excel tools
  - o Single-channel models
    - M/M/1 model
    - M/G/1 model
    - G/M/1
    - G/G/1 model
  - o Multiple-channel models
  - o Single-channel, multiple-phase manufacturing model
- Random number approximations of probability distributions

Little's Law,[1] $L = \lambda W$ or $L_q = \lambda W_q$, is arguably the most useful concept that waiting line analysts have in their toolboxes. It holds true regardless of the probability distributions used to describe the arrival and service rates for a waiting line; it is also independent of the number of servers used. Its primary value is that data for determining L, L_q, and λ can be collected easily in most businesses, which allows easy calculations of W and W_q. Knowing all these values then allows an easy determination of the average service time for many of the waiting line models.

The following discussion on collecting waiting line data gives some examples of the versatility of Little's Law.

Waiting Line Data Collection

Having actual operational data about your business is necessary for being able to use queuing analysis models effectively. In many situations, the classic exponential distributions for arrival and service rates do not represent your business as well as another standard probability distribution or a discrete distribution tailored to fit your typical business conditions. To assess the need for choosing an alternate probability distribution for either the arrival rate or the service rate, you need to collect enough data to guide you in that choice and provide some of the average performance values for the appropriate waiting line model.

One class exercise that I have asked my process management students to do is to collect data while observing the waiting line behavior at various campus coffee shops. They are expected to analyze that data and use it in a subsequent waiting line simulation exercise. A sample data sheet from that exercise is shown in Figure 7.1. While these student exercises are specific to coffee shops, the general data collection and simulation approach is applicable to a wide variety of waiting line scenarios. We will discuss their work in more detail in the examples presented in this chapter.

We will collect data only about line lengths and arrival rates. Observing actual waiting and service times is much more difficult and not needed because we can derive waiting times from the line length and arrival data. Service times are a bit trickier but can be estimated for most scenarios once we have the waiting time values. For good data, the following guidelines should be followed:

- Select a suitably short collection period for each pair of line length and arrival rate values. For low arrival rates, where there is typically enough time between arrivals to count the number of people in the facility being served and waiting for service, it is better to record the amount of time between each arrival to

BA 302 Assignment 3, Part 1: Waiting Line Performance Data Collection

Coffee Shop Chosen: _____   Location: _____

Date: 4/4/11 _____   Time(s) Started: 11:33 _____ _____

Team Members: _____   Section: _____

Total Time	# Customers entering during this 5-minute period	# Customers in Line and being served at end of this 5-minute period	# Servers working directly with customers during this 5-minute period	Any Observations during this 5-minute period
5 min	II	2	0	1	
10 min	IIII	5	0	1	
15 min	IIII IIII II	12	3	1	
20 min	IIII IIII	9	4	1	
25 min	IIII IIII II	12	5		
30 min	IIII IIII III	13	8	1	
35 min	III	5	6		
40 min	IIII	5	1	1	
45 min	IIII II	6	6	1	
50 min	IIII	4	2	1	
55 min	I	1	0	1	
60 min	I	1	0	1	
65 min	IIII	4	0	1	
70 min	IIII	5	2	1	
75 min	IIII	4	2	1	
80 min	III	3	0	1	
85 min	IIII III	8	2	1	
90 min	IIII II	7	3	1	
95 min	I	1	0	1	
100 min	IIII	4	1	1	
105 min	IIII	4	1	1	
110 min	II	2	0	1	
115 min	IIII II	7	2	1	
120 min	IIII	4	1	1	
Total #		130	44		
Average #		5.42	1.8		

Figure 7.1. A data collection form for a coffee shop waiting line process study. The length of the data collection period is 5 minutes.

determine the arrival rate. If the arrival rate is too fast to count the number of customers in the facility between arrivals, then select a fixed time segment that is at least three or four times as long as it typically takes to count the number of customers in line. Record the number of arrivals during each period and the number of customers in the facility at the end or the beginning of each period. For the student's coffee shop exercise, the fixed time period was 5 minutes.

- *Hint:* It is useful to have one person note the arrivals and another person count the customers. Trying to do both at the same time can be challenging for a single person, particularly if the business is busy. Mechanical counters and stopwatches are useful but unnecessary tools if you have a good watch and paper and pencil for making tally marks.

- If you want to determine average service times, note the number of servers on duty during each recording period. If not, you can ignore this information (more about this decision later).
- Unless you have good reason to believe that your arrival rate is relatively constant throughout the working day, record the starting time for each record period. This is not usually required for production lines, where the production schedule normally ensures a relatively steady arrival rate.
- If your business has different service classes (express lanes, commercial customers only, etc.), be sure to collect data separately for each class if you want to derive service time and arrival rates per class. In this case, for more accurate data, avoid having servers in one class serve customers from another class when those servers have an idle period.
- Pay close attention to the measurement units. In Figure 7.1, the average line length is independent of the length of the collection period. Not so for the average arrival rate shown; that average is dependent on the number of arrivals per period. The form also clearly states that the line values are for L, not L_q.

Example 7.1. Data Collection for an M/M/1 Model

This example demonstrates how we can use the information collected in Figure 7.1, where the duration of each data collection period is 5 minutes and 2 hours' worth of data is collected. For a business application, we would want more data, particularly if we wanted to also develop a more accurate discrete probability distribution that we could use to represent the arrival rate in a simulation model.

First, the students added the 24 line values they recorded for a total of 44 and divided that total by 24 to get an average line length of 1.833. However, they incorrectly added the line values because the total should be 50, not 44 (did you catch it?), so the correct line length is 50/24 = 2.083 = L. This error indicates that their other results should also be checked. Sure enough, there is one more error where they translated 5 tally marks for the 50-minute period into the number 4 instead of the correct value of 5. Hence, the correct total number of arrivals is 131, not 130. This gives an average arrival rate per collection period of $131/24 = 5.458$ arrivals every 5 minutes. Because we also know that the total time for the data collection took 120 minutes, we can also divide the total number of arrivals by that time to get the rate per minute $= 1.0916/$minute or 65.5 customers per hour.

Why did we spend time here dealing with mathematical errors? First, we are emphasizing that manual data collection methods are prone to mathematical errors because of the sheer volume of numbers involved. Second, even small errors, particularly when they occur in only one variable, can result in considerable analysis and simulation errors. It is always good to double-check your data before investing more analysis time in using it.

Using Little's Law, the average total time W spent in the coffee shop is therefore $L/\lambda = 2.083 \div 1.0916/$minute $= 1.908$ minutes or 114.5 seconds, a respectable time for students who want to just pop in for a quick coffee before going to class.

Now we did not collect waiting-in-line data for L_q, but we can still obtain that value, the average time spent waiting in line, and also the average service time with what we have because the coffee shop line can be described as an $M/M/1$ model. For that model, $W = 1/(\mu - \lambda) = L/\lambda$ and $W_q = W - (1/\mu)$. Because we now have L and λ from the data collection and W using Little's Law, we can use the first equation to solve for μ and then use the second equation to solve for W_q, which in turn will give us L_q using Little's Law again. Running the numbers, we obtain $\mu = \lambda + (1/W) = 1.0916/$minute $+ 1/1.908$ minutes $= 1.6157$ customers per minute. Therefore, $W_q = 1.908$ minutes $- (1/1.6157)$ minutes $= 1.289$ minutes and $L_q = \lambda W_q = 1.0916 \times 1.289 = 1.407$ customers.

In this example, there is not enough information (should have at least 50 values per set and at least 10 sets taken at different times during the week) to determine whether a different probability distribution than the usual exponential distribution should be used for the arrival rate. Although we were able to determine the average service rate, there are no individual service time values to use for determining a service time distribution. We would need to collect actual individual service time values to do that; this could be done by having a staff member time each transaction for a long enough time to get at least 50 values, more when the variability of the values is high. Similarly, if we desire a more accurate estimate of the interarrival time distribution, we need to also collect at least 50 or more values for the length of time between each successive customer arrival. We will go into these data requirements in some more detail in Example 7.2. *Note:* Unlike line length values, arrival and service time values can be collected in any order and combined for the purpose of analyzing actual probability distributions because both values are memoryless.

Discrete Probability Distributions

A valuable characteristic of simulation models is that they can work with either continuous distributions, like the ones we have discussed for various queuing models, or discrete distributions based on collections of actual data. The difference in the approach is that we use random numbers to calculate the values for the simulation from the mathematical functions that describe the continuous distributions, or we use those random numbers in a lookup table to select a discrete value from the histogram of the data collection. Examples 7.2 and 7.3 illustrate these two approaches using some more data collected from my coffee shop data collection assignments.

Example 7.2. Continuous Distribution Determination
The data collection time for a different campus coffee shop from that used in Example 7.1 was increased to 500 minutes to enable the collection of 100 data values, keeping 5-minute data periods for both arrival rate and the line length. Graphs of both values collected are shown in Figure 7.2. This length of time is consistent with an 8-hour day. Using the same types of calculations shown in Example 7.1 for this larger data set, we obtain $\lambda = 1.470$/minute or 7.35 arrivals every 5 minutes, $L = 3.260$, $W = 2.218$ minutes, and $\mu = 1.921$/minute. Looking at the values versus time in Figure 7.2, we can observe that average values rarely occur and certainly not at the same time, line

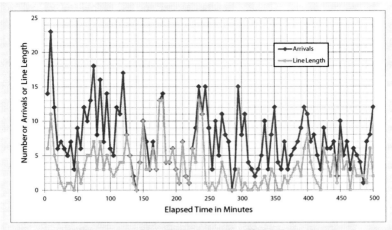

*Figure 7.2. Arrival and line length data collected over a
500-minute interval for a coffee shop waiting line process study.
The length of the data collection period is 5 minutes.*

lengths are less than or equal to the arrival rates at any given time, line
lengths sometimes decrease when arrival rates decrease (when a cluster
of short service times occurs), and both values can be considerably
larger or smaller than the average values. Like Figure 2.3, this reem-
phasizes the fact that the average values obtained from waiting line
model equations are not good indicators of what a typical customer
will observe.

You must be careful in using the data. The values for L and λ were
calculated using individual pieces of data, and a histogram of that data
will represent the true distribution of that data. Calculating the average interarrival time for a period by dividing 5 minutes by the number
of arrivals for that period gives an average interarrival time for a data
sample that contains one or more pieces of individual data. Similarly,
calculating the service rate for a period is an average of the service
times that took place during that period and thus is also considered
a sample of data because it contains one or more pieces of individual
data in its value. That is, each individual arrival has its own interarrival
and service times that are being treated as being the same value during a data collection period when they actually differ for each arrival.
Complicating the validity of the service time data is that some of the

individual service times in one period are for some of the arrivals from the previous period.

Because the Central Limit Theorem states that the distribution of sample averages approaches that of a normal distribution as the number of samples increases, this means that histograms of interarrival and service times obtained in the way discussed previously will not give us an idea of what their underlying probability distributions are. *We have to have histograms of raw data to do that.* This is the reason for also collecting individual service and interarrival times and is a key part of the discussion with students when they do this exercise.

So how do we proceed with the data we have? First, we must recognize that the line length values are results, not inputs or drivers to the situation. What we need to focus on are the drivers: arrivals and service times. We will begin with a histogram[2] of the arrival data and see what it can tell us. We have some choices to make in setting up the histogram. The choice of bin size for sorting the arrival values is important. A large bin size reduces the number of bins required but requires counting the occurrences of a range of arrival values in each bin. A small bin size allows assigning a bin to record the number of occurrences for each distinctive arrival value but requires a large number of bins. In general, the number of bins should be roughly between 10% and 20% of the number of values to be plotted if you want to look at the shape of the distribution. Reviewing the arrival values plotted in Figure 7.2, I chose a bin range from 0 to 23 (minimum to maximum arrival values) and a bin size of 1. This bin size allows me to determine the number of occurrences (frequency) for each distinctive arrival value. Because we have 100 values for this situation, the percentage of bins is 23%. I also asked the histogram function to plot the cumulative percentage of the arrival frequencies. The result is shown in Figure 7.3.

The frequency bars indicate that the arrival distribution approximates a Poisson distribution, and the cumulative percentage plot verifies this assumption by closely approximating the cumulative distribution function for an exponential distribution. To further verify this conclusion, we can check to see if our average arrival rate value corresponds to the 63.3% point[3] on the curve. The histogram shows

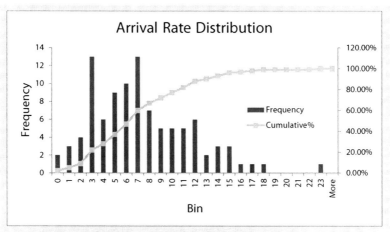

*Figure 7.3. Arrival rate histogram for data shown in Figure 7.2.
The bin size is 1; the bin number represents the arrival rate value
counted in that bin. For example, bin 4 shows the number of times
only 4 arrivals occurred during a 5-minute period.*

that value to be somewhere between 7 and 8 arrivals per period. Our
value is 7.35 arrivals every 5 minutes, a close agreement. This allows us
to use an exponential distribution with an average arrival rate of 1.47
arrivals per minute for this coffee shop.

This outcome is not unexpected because an exponential distribution is often a good representation of real-life arrival behavior.
Thus we can use a formula with a random number as its input to
simulate arrival rates and interarrival times in our simulation for
this coffee shop business. Such formulas are discussed later in this
chapter.

Example 7.3. Discrete Distribution Determination
In an attempt to determine what service-time probability distribution
we should use for a simulation of our coffee shop business, we will try
a little experiment where we determine the *average* service rate for each
5-minute data collection period by using the arrival rate and the line
length for that period to determine the waiting time for that period,
which then should allow us to calculate an average service time for

that period using the equation $\mu = (1/W) + \lambda$ from the $M/M/1$ model. Averaging those 100 average service rate values, we obtain an average rate of 1.94/minute. Wait a minute! That does not agree with the 1.921/minute value derived at the beginning of Example 7.2. What did we do wrong?

Because the 1.921 value for μ was derived from the averages for λ and L using equations that account for probability distributions and the 1.94 value is based on only a global average of sample averages for μ, the methods are not exactly equivalent. Remembering that the average service rate for each period is partly based on service times for arrivals that occurred in previous periods but were not serviced in those periods, the 1.921 value is the more accurate estimate because averaging over the total time of 500 minutes minimizes those effects.

Because we do not have actual individual service times to determine the most appropriate service distribution for our simulation, can we just use an exponential distribution with an average service rate of 1.921/minute as suggested by the waiting line models? Recognizing that most service operations have a minimum service time, a pure exponential distribution is not appropriate for this simulation because it allows for a relatively high percentage of short service times. A normal distribution could be used for fairly standard services, but for a typical coffee shop, there can be some fairly long service times associated with large orders or complicated coffee requests.

Recalling Example 4.1, it would be better if we start with an Erlang distribution that can be adjusted to fit a variety of service distributions by varying its k value (the number of independent exponential distributions that are added together to form the overall distribution). Use k = 2 as a starting point for our simulation and compare its predictions with our actual values. If there is close agreement, we are good to go. If not, we can try different k values to achieve a better result. If that fails, we need to collect actual individual service time data to determine a more suitable distribution or use that data to describe a discrete probability distribution that the simulation can use in a lookup table.

Let's look at the service rate values that we calculated for each 5-minute period for the coffee shop in Figures 7.2 and 7.3. The histogram is shown in Figure 7.4. Keep in mind that decimal values will be counted in the bin preceding the next higher integer; that is, a value of 9.37 will be counted in bin 9.

As might be expected, given how the values were calculated, the distribution and the cumulative percentage curve are more ragged. Two values are not counted in the available bins, and there are two occurrences of zero service rates because there were zero arrivals for two periods. In actual practice, these are nonexistent values and must be ignored because service rate only has meaning when associated with a customer. The one occurrence for bin 13 indicates that the associated service time $(1/\mu)$ is an unlikely service time for this coffee shop. Discrete distributions have an advantage over continuous distributions in that anomalies like this can be accounted for in simulations.

To convert this information into a discrete distribution for use in simulations, we need to do the following:

1. List the valid recorded values in order of value in one column. Ignore the zero service rate value for this example. List each distinct value only once.
2. List the associated number of occurrences for each value in an adjacent column to the right of the first column. Total the number of occurrences for all listed values at the bottom of that column.
3. In a third column adjacent and to the right of the second column, calculate the cumulative percentage for the occurrences, beginning at the top and ending with 100% at the bottom.
4. In a fourth column adjacent and to the *left* of the first column, assign ranges of random numbers to each value in the first column by specifying a random number equal to the cumulative percentage for the previous value. Although this may be confusing, it supports the format for lookup tables in Excel.
5. Use the columns created in steps 1 and 4 for creating a vertical lookup table in Excel, where random numbers can be used to select values according to their probability of occurring.

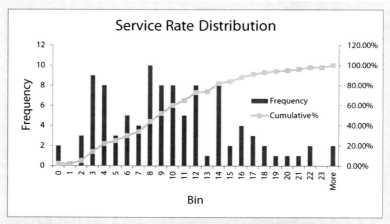

*Figure 7.4. Service rate histogram for data shown in Figure 7.2.
The bin size is 1; the bin number represents the service rate value
counted in that bin. For example, bin 4 shows the number of times
only 4 customers were serviced during a 5-minute period.*

Figure 7.5 shows the result of this process using the service rate
values shown in Figure 7.4. Unlike the histogram in Figure 7.4, this
process allows us to use exact decimal values for our discrete distribution rather than numbers rounded off according to bin size.

As an example of how the result in Figure 7.5 is used in a simulation, when a service time needs to be assigned to a new customer
according to this discrete service rate distribution, the Excel expression
in Equation 7.1 is used to obtain that service time. To help understand the cell assignments in the expression, the cell containing the
title "Minimum Random Number Assigned" has a cell address of K4
in the spreadsheet.

The VLOOKUP function for a simulated service time for this coffee shop (remembering that service time = $1/\mu$ and that μ here is based
on data for a 5-minute period) is as follows:

$$= 5/(\text{VLOOKUP}(\text{RAND}(),\$K\$6{:}\$L\$47,2,\text{TRUE})) \qquad (7.1)$$

For a random number equal to 0.343681, this expression finds a
service rate of 7.5 customers every 5 minutes and returns an average
service time of 0.666667 minutes.

Minimum Random Number Assigned	Service Rate per Period Sorted	Count per Value	Cumulative Percentage
	0.00	Ignore	
0	1.50	1	1.02%
0.0102	2.00	2	3.06%
0.0306	3.00	9	12.24%
0.1224	4.00	8	20.41%
0.2041	5.00	3	23.47%
0.2347	6.00	5	28.57%
0.2857	6.67	1	29.59%
0.2959	7.00	3	32.65%
0.3265	7.50	5	37.76%
0.3776	8.00	5	42.86%
0.4286	8.17	1	43.88%
0.4388	8.40	1	44.90%
0.4490	8.75	3	47.96%
0.4796	9.00	3	51.02%
0.5102	9.33	3	54.08%
0.5408	10.00	5	59.18%
0.5918	10.50	2	61.22%
0.6122	10.67	2	63.27%
0.6327	11.00	1	64.29%
0.6429	11.25	2	66.33%
0.6633	11.43	1	67.35%
0.6735	12.00	5	72.45%
0.7245	12.38	1	73.47%
0.7347	13.50	1	74.49%
0.7449	13.75	2	76.53%
0.7653	14.00	5	81.63%
0.8163	14.40	1	82.65%
0.8265	15.00	1	83.67%
0.8367	15.08	1	84.69%
0.8469	15.60	1	85.71%
0.8571	16.00	2	87.76%
0.8776	16.15	1	88.78%
0.8878	16.33	1	89.80%
0.8980	16.80	1	90.82%
0.9082	18.00	2	92.86%
0.9286	18.29	1	93.88%
0.9388	20.00	1	94.90%
0.9490	20.57	1	95.92%
0.9592	21.25	1	96.94%
0.9694	22.00	1	97.96%
0.9796	25.09	1	98.98%
0.9898	30.00	1	100.00%
		98	

Figure 7.5. Discrete distribution and lookup table.

Simulation Models

Setting up simulation models for waiting lines is simpler than for some other types of simulations. Because waiting lines are time based with a defined sequence of steps or phases, all the simulation has to do is keep track of when each customer or item enters the queue and how much time a customer spends at each step in the waiting line sequence. The tricky part is that the movement of customers that enter the queue later can be affected by the movements of customers who entered the queue earlier. When the time between successive arrivals is short, the probability of this occurring obviously increases.

Figure 7.6 shows an example of the sequence of events for a simple M/M/1 model with one service operation. The vertical axis represents the number of customers who have entered the queue, and the horizontal axis represents the passage of time. A horizontal bar represents each customer; the length of the bar represents how long the customer spent in the service system, with the left end representing when he or she entered and the right end when he or she left. This bar is normally divided into two parts, one shaded gray to represent how long the customer waits in the queue for service and the other colored black to represent how long the service took. The entry times are determined by the arrival distribution associated with the type of queue being simulated, and their service times are determined

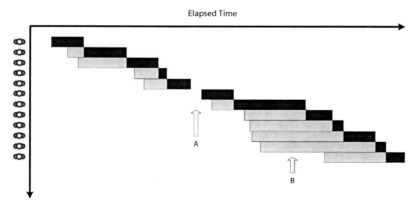

Figure 7.6. Time-lapse diagram of customer arrivals into an M/M/1 queuing system beginning at the top of the diagram for the first customer and showing the amount of time each customer spent waiting (gray rectangle) and being served (black rectangle).

by the service distribution appropriate for the service being simulated. Of interest in Figure 7.6 are the conditions when there are no customers in the system, indicated by the arrow labeled A, and when there are five customers in the system, indicated by the arrow labeled B.

If Figure 7.6 is compared to the look of a typical computer spreadsheet, you should be able to recognize the similarities where the rows and columns of the spreadsheet could be used to represent the activities taking place and determine some of the performance values. Figure 7.7 shows an example of how this can be done and provides a template for a basic simulation module for waiting line analysis.

Like the diagram in Figure 7.6, the simulation model template in Figure 7.7 addresses each customer or unit in an order going down the sheet and determines the various performance times in an order moving toward the right. The Arrival Time column is where the entry time for the customer is entered in the template. This time is determined by adding the interarrival time for customer n to the arrival time recorded for customer n − 1. The interarrival time is chosen at random from the arrival distribution chosen for the model using an appropriate method that determines an interarrival value based on a random number input generated by the spreadsheet program. A similar method is done to select a service time for a customer using a different random number. When using continuous probability distributions, the method uses the random number to calculate a corresponding value according to that distribution as described in appendix D. When using discrete probability distributions, the method uses the random number to select a corresponding value using a lookup table similar to that shown in Figure 7.5.

The Service Starts column determines when the service begins for customer n by comparing customer n's arrival time with the Service Ends time for customer n − 1. If that time is greater than customer n's arrival time, it becomes the start of service time for customer n; if not, the start of service time is the same as customer n's arrival time. The Service Ends column is the randomly chosen service time for a customer added to that customer's start of service time.

Hence the arrival times in the simulation are solely determined by the arrival distribution chosen for the simulation. But the service start and end times are affected by both the previous customer's service end time and the service distribution chosen.

Basic Single-Channel, Single-Phase Model M/M/1 Simulation

Conditions:

Clock starts at zero.

No customers (units) are waiting in line at the beginning.

Arrival and service times are exponentially distributed.

Times are in minutes.

Number in line awaiting service includes the latest customer (unit) to arrive.

Slack time is time server waits after previous customer (unit) departs until current customer (unit) arrives.

Inputs:

Average Arrival Rate =   per minute

Average Service Rate =   per minute

Unit	Arrival Time	Service Starts	Service Ends	Wait in Line W_q	Time in System W	Service Time	Number in System L	Slack Time
1								
2								
3								
4								
5								

Figure 7.7. Basic spreadsheet simulation template for an M/M/1 queuing system.

W_q is merely the difference between a customer's arrival time and when service starts for that customer. W is merely the difference between the service end time and the arrival time. Slack time is any positive difference between the service end time for customer n − 1 and the start of service for customer n (occurs only when customer n arrives *after* the service for customer n − 1 is completed). This time is idle time and can be used to determine P_0 for the simulation.

Obtaining L is a bit tricky but not difficult. If you observe the situation indicated by arrow B in Figure 7.6, you can see that the number of people in the system after customer n arrives is the number of customers, including customer n, whose start of service times are greater than customer n's arrival time. So all you have to do is count the number of service start times for customers n, n − 1, n − 2, n − 3 . . . 3, 2, and 1 that are greater than the arrival time for customer n. If you desire an L_q result that indicates what a potential customer would see when entering your business, delete customer n in your L_q calculations. The Excel COUNTIF function is very useful for the L determination. Count the range of cells containing the service completion times for all the previous customers using the following criteria statement in the COUNTIF expression:

">"&(cell address for customer n's arrival time)

There is an example in appendix D of using the COUNTIF function for the results shown in Figure 7.8.

You should see that this model works for all choices of arrival and service distributions. All you need to do is alter the algorithms for selecting arrival times and service times to fit your chosen distribution. Hence, M/D/1, M/G/1, G/M/1, G/G/1, D/M/1, and D/G/1 models can be accommodated.

The last two models with deterministic (D) arrival distributions can be used to simulate appointment-based arrival distributions, such as the health-care situation discussed in Example 6.5. Using an exponential or Erlang distribution to describe service time, you can then evaluate different appointment durations by using constant interarrival times equal to those durations. You can even accommodate potential late or early arrivals by adding a small variation value to each interarrival time. That value could be normally distributed, or it could be based on a discrete distribution created from actual early or late arrival data.

Basic Single-Channel, Single-Phase Model M/M/1 Simulation

Conditions:

Clock starts at zero.
No customers (units) are waiting in line at the beginning.
Arrival and service times are exponentially distributed.
Times are in minutes.
Number in line awaiting service includes the latest customer (unit) to arrive.
Slack time is time server waits after previous customer (unit) departs until current customer (unit) arrives.

Inputs:

Average Arrival Rate = 1.47 per minute
Average Service Rate = 1.921 per minute

Unit	Arrival Time	Service Starts	Service Ends	Wait in Line W_q	Time in System W	Service Time	Number in System L	Slack Time
1	0.382	0.382	1.357	0.000	0.975	0.975	0.000	0.382
2	1.830	1.830	2.187	0.000	0.357	0.357	0.000	0.473
3	2.518	2.518	2.800	0.000	0.282	0.282	0.000	0.331
4	4.026	4.026	5.226	0.000	1.200	1.200	0.000	1.226
5	4.670	5.226	5.526	0.556	0.856	0.300	1.000	0.000
6	5.210	5.526	5.861	0.316	0.651	0.335	2.000	0.000
7	5.324	5.861	6.323	0.537	0.999	0.462	2.000	0.000
8	5.461	6.323	7.510	0.862	2.049	1.187	3.000	0.000
9	6.392	7.510	7.763	1.118	1.372	0.254	1.000	0.000
10	6.604	7.763	7.769	1.160	1.165	0.006	2.000	0.000
11	7.409	7.769	8.904	0.360	1.495	1.135	3.000	0.000
12	8.385	8.904	9.036	0.519	0.651	0.132	1.000	0.000
13	8.511	9.036	9.162	0.524	0.651	0.127	2.000	0.000
14	8.775	9.162	9.450	0.388	0.676	0.288	3.000	0.000
15	9.174	9.450	10.072	0.276	0.898	0.622	1.000	0.000

Figure 7.8. The basic simulation module template from Figure 7.7 set up for an M/M/1 model using the data from Examples 7.2 and 7.3.

Random Number Approximations
of Probability Distributions

Many arrival and service distributions are in a form that allows the use of random numbers to select a value from the distribution in accordance with its probability of occurring. Random numbers generated by many spreadsheet programs are in the form of a decimal value varying from one significant digit greater than 0 to one significant digit less than 1, for example, 0.00000001 to 0.99999999. These values have a uniform distribution; that is, the probability of any random number occurring is equally likely. This means that they can be used as probability values without introducing any bias to the selection.

Consider the probability density function for the exponential distribution is given by $f(t) = \alpha e^{-\alpha t}$ for $t \geq 0$, where α can represent either λ or μ, and t is the time between arrivals or successive service starts (same as service times). The cumulative distribution function for this probability density function represents the cumulative area underneath the curve represented by the probability density function as a function of t. This function is described by the equation

$$P(t) = 1 - e^{-\alpha t} \text{ for } t \geq 0. \qquad (7.2)$$

For an exponential distribution, a plot of the cumulative distribution function is the vertical inverse of the plot for the probability density function. That is, the first plot increases from 0 to a maximum value of 1, and the other plot decreases from a maximum value of 1 to 0. Equation 7.2 gives us the probability that the time between intervals will be t or less. Now if we could substitute a random number (RN) for $f(t)$, in effect using the random number to represent a given probability value, we should be able to solve Equation 7.2 for the t value correlating to that probability value. The result is that we can use that equation to give us intervals of time using random numbers as the inputs:

$$P(t) = RN = 1 - e^{-\alpha t} \text{ for } t \geq 0. \qquad (7.3)$$

Rearranging Equation 7.3, we first obtain $e^{-\alpha t} = 1 - RN$. Then taking the natural logarithms of both sides gives us the result: $-\alpha t = \ln(1 - RN)$. Solving for t, we arrive at the equation we want to use in our simulation model for obtaining an interarrival time or service time described by an exponential distribution.

$$t = -(1/\alpha) \times \ln(1 - RN).$$

Recognizing that $(1 - RN)$ is also a random number with the same range of values,

$$t = -\alpha^{-1} \times \ln(RN). \tag{7.4}$$

Equation 7.4 is used to provide the results shown in Figure 7.8 for a simulation that uses the values collected for Examples 7.2 and 7.3. A list of other equations that have been derived for different probability distributions is provided in appendix D.

Finally, considering the basic module shown in Figure 7.9 as a building block for simulations with a set of inputs (arrivals) and a set of outputs (departing customers or completed items), you can mix and match these to address more complicated waiting line situations by observing a few rules, as follows:

1. Like state diagrams, each module can be considered as a state with inputs equaling outputs. The state of the module can be described by its inventory (line length).
2. Like the probability distributions that describe arrival rates and service times, each module's internal actions are essentially independent of each other, provided that there is no sharing of resources (servers, equipment) with other modules.
3. When the outputs of a module are divided among two or more subsequent modules or when the inputs to a module come

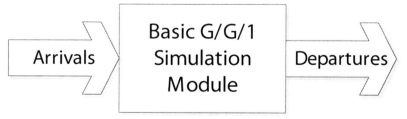

Figure 7.9. The basic G/G/1 simulation module represented as a building block for larger-scale simulations. Inside this module is a simulation as shown in Figure 7.7 with arrival times tallied in a column on the left and departure times listed in a column on the right.

Figure 7.10. The basic traffic modules required as building blocks for more complex simulations. The services performed by these modules take essentially zero time and typically are combining or sorting algorithms.

from more than one source, separate types of simulation modules must be developed to manage this traffic, as illustrated in Figure 7.10. This is not difficult if the various input or output components can be defined by fixed percentages or known probability distributions.

4. Single-line configurations for multiple servers are easier to model than parallel-line configurations, but both require a traffic module, as shown in Figure 7.11a and Figure 7.11b. One directs the next customer in a single line to the next available server; the other distributes incoming customers to the available parallel lines according to whatever rule is desired. For example, in typical bank or governmental office applications the rule is likely to be to the parallel line with the least number of customers waiting in line. Another example is directing incoming customers according to their class or priority.

5. An advantage of simulation is that modules can have different service distributions, which are useful when simulating multiple-phase lines or customizing a multiple-server situation where not every server can be assumed to have the same service capability. For example, one can simulate the effect of dedicating one server to standardized services in a two- or three-server situation as compared to all servers handling the full range of services.

6. When one module's output is the input to a following module, the arrival distribution for the following model is the same as the output distribution for the preceding model, as shown for the production line simulation in Figure 7.12. Note that the output distribution of a previous module is *not* the same as that module's service time

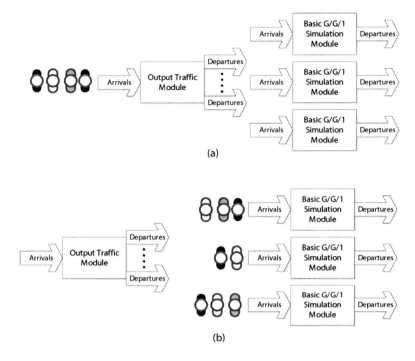

Figure 7.11. Simulation module configurations for the two different multiple-server line configurations: (a) single-line multiple-server simulation and (b) parallel-line multiple-server simulation.

distribution unless the server in that module is continually busy, as may be the case in a production line situation.

It can be seen that spreadsheet implementations of these modules for different simulations can be pretty straightforward. For example, a multiple step production process can use the first few columns of the spreadsheet as shown in Figure 7.7 for the first step, the next set of columns for the second step set up in the same way as for the first step with the Service Ends column values for the first step also acting as the Arrival Time values for the second step and so forth. Finally, some useful references for further study about spreadsheet simulation methods are Laguna and Marklund (2005), chapter 6; Winston (2004); and Weida et al. (2001).

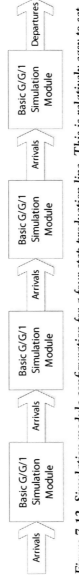

Figure 7.12. Simulation module configuration for a four-step production line. This is relatively easy to set up in a spreadsheet and allows different service distributions at each step. If a given step has inadequate capacity, one or more modules can be used in parallel for that step, with the departures from the previous module being easily divided among the parallel modules. Their outputs can then be combined for the input to the following step's module.

APPENDIX A

Glossary

Arrival. A customer or item entering a line or queue for service or further processing.

Arrival distribution. The variability in the number of arrivals per some selected period of time. This variability can be represented by selected probability distributions to best fit the particular situation, with the Poisson distribution being most commonly used.

Arrival rate. The average number of arrivals per some selected period of time. This continuous value can have a decimal component for small arrival rates, but it is often rounded to whole numbers for larger rates. This value is represented by the Greek lambda (λ) in waiting line equations. Some typical values are 30 products per day, 18 customers per hour, or 1.6 cars every 15 minutes.

Back office. A term that denotes those activities in a service process where direct contact with the customer is not required for their completion.

Balance equation. A useful condition in waiting line analysis that can be used to derive several performance measures. Consider a state n where there are n customers in the system and the queue is in a steady state. At this time, the inputs to state n are equal to the outputs from state n. That is, Rate($\rightarrow$ n) = Rate($\leftarrow$ n). This allows the creation of a set of equations, one per state, which then can be mathematically manipulated to determine the probability of existence for each state. Given those probabilities, average line lengths and, subsequently, the average waiting times can be determined.

Balking. Refusal of a customer to enter a line the customer considers too long. It is a waiting line cost, particularly if the customer decides to never return. Balking is also an example of a state-dependent rate in which the probability of its occurrence is related to the length of the waiting line observed by the next arrival.

Birth and death process. A continuous Markov chain that is occasionally abbreviated by some authors as BDP. In queuing analysis, its state diagram can be used to determine how long it will take for a queuing situation to reach a steady state of behavior. When that condition exists, it can be used to derive the various waiting line performance formulas.

Blocking. Not allowing a customer to enter a line because of limited capacity. One example is when all the lines to a call center are busy. It is a waiting line cost.

Calling population. The pool of possible arrivals. For most customer services, the calling population is assumed to be infinite; but for some situations, this population has a limited or fixed size that affects subsequent arrival rates over time. Some may wonder why the adjective *calling* is used; the likely reason is because early waiting line analysis was focused on the needs of telephone companies to provide their users (callers) acceptable service at the lowest cost.

Central Limit Theorem. A law that states that the distribution of sample averages approaches that of a normal distribution as the number of samples increases. This occurs regardless of the nature of the underlying distribution of the individual data values from which the samples were taken.

Channel. A single server for a waiting line.

Coefficient of variation. The standard deviation/mean ratio for a distribution. This ratio is a key component of the Pollaczek-Khintchine formula used for general distributions in waiting line analysis equations. See also *Pollaczek-Khintchine (P-K) formula*.

Coxian distribution.[1] A special case of a phase-type distribution where the requirement for entering the first phase in a sequence of phases is relaxed so that the sequence can be entered at any phase. A typical application would be sequencing analysis in a job shop.

Dequeue (or sometimes deque). A concept usually reserved for computer applications, where a customer can be added or subtracted from either the head or the tail of the line.

Deterministic. Having a predictable value with a very narrow range of variance. As a result, deterministic variables do not require probability distributions to describe their behavior in analysis methods and can usually be represented by a constant value. In the context of this monograph, some examples are the service time for an automated process, arrival times created by a production schedule, the number of servers, finite population size, and finite capacity. See also *stochastic*.

Erlang distribution.[2] A special case of the gamma distribution where the shape factor k is restricted to integer values. The shape factor represents the number of independent exponential distributions added together to form the distribution. When k = 1, the distribution defaults to a single exponential distribution.

Erlang loss function. Also referred to as the Erlang B expression, can be used to estimate how many customers are turned away (blocked) by limited capacity (no waiting positions, e.g., all lines are busy at a call center). The Erlang C expression, which is more complicated, assumes that there are infinite waiting positions. It is used to estimate the probability that a customer will arrive, find that all servers are currently busy, and then get into line to wait until a server becomes available.

FCFS. First come, first serve. The most common priority rule for a waiting line.

FIFO. First in, first out. Same as FCFS.

Front office. A term used to denote those activities in a service process where direct contact with a customer is necessary for their completion.

Interarrival distribution. The variability in the interarrival time, which can be represented by selected probability distributions that best fit the particular situation, with the exponential distribution being the most commonly used.

Interarrival time. The time between arrivals in a waiting line. The average value is the inverse of the arrival rate (i.e., $1/\lambda$). The sequence of interarrival times is often characterized as a Markovian process.

Jockeying. Changing from a slowly moving line to another line that is perceived to be moving faster in a multiple-channel situation using separate lines for each server.

Kendall notation.[3] A shorthand method for identifying different waiting line models using designated symbols for the arrival rate distribution, the service time distribution, the number of channels, the line length limitation, the calling population size, and the priority rule.

Line length. The number of customers or items in a queue. The average line length is characterized by two continuous values: the average number in line (L_q) awaiting service and the total number in the system (L), which includes those being served.

Little's Law. An observation that the ratio between given average line length and waiting time values is characterized by the average arrival rate value for all waiting line models ($\lambda = L/W$).

Makespan. The total time required to complete a group of jobs in manufacturing. For waiting lines, this corresponds to the total amount of time required to process a group of waiting customers.

Markovian process.[4] A process characterized by a sequence of random variables (x_1, x_2, x_3, . . .) whose order is indicated by increasing values of a parameter, usually time in waiting line scenarios, and having the property that any prediction of the next value of the sequence (x_n) can be based on knowing just the current state or previous value (x_{n-1}). That is, the future value of such a variable is independent of the values of all of the previous values but the last one.

Memoryless. A condition where a value is independent of any previous value. That is, it can be said that the value has no memory of any preceding values.

PASTA. An abbreviation for the statement "Poisson arrivals see time averages." In other words, for any line with exponentially distributed interarrival times, each customer has the same probability of seeing a given line condition. Therefore, the average of what a frequent customer observes will be the same as the average determined by waiting line analysis.

Phase. A single step for a service with no intervening waiting lines.

Phase-type distribution. A distribution for one or more phases in sequence whose intervening arrival rates can be characterized by interrelated Poisson distributions. These complex expressions are beyond the scope of this monograph and are mentioned here only for readers wishing to delve further into analytical solutions.

Pollaczek-Khintchine (P-K) formula.[5] An expression developed to determine the average delay in a single-channel waiting line for any general service time distribution. All that is needed to be known about the distribution is its mean and variance. The generalized formula in the context of the terms used in this monograph is as follows:

$$W_q = \left(\frac{1}{\rho}\right) \times \frac{\rho}{1-\rho} \times \frac{C_{1/\rho}^2}{2}.$$

POS. Point of sale. Useful information regarding the nature of services performed and the types of customers served can be gained by a business analyzing its POS data.

Priority queue. A waiting line where the order in which arrivals are served is different from first come, first served. Different preemptive and nonpreemptive rules can be applied within a single line, or separate lines can be established for different priorities.

Priority rule. A waiting line discipline for serving arrivals after they enter the queue. The most commonly used rule is first come, first served; but in other more urgent situations, the most important needs will prevail, such as in emergency room queues. See also *priority queue*.

Probability of zero customers. The percentage of time when a service business will have no customers in line and being served. This value is represented by the symbol P_0 in most waiting line formulas and is important to managers because it allows an estimate of how much time servers can be available to work on other activities not directly related to customer service.

Queue. A line of people waiting for some service or a sequence of items waiting for the next process step. This term is more widely used outside the United States and is considered synonymous with the term *waiting line*.

Reneging. Leaving a line before being served after having spent some time in it. If a customer is dissatisfied enough to not come back, it is a significant waiting line cost.

Service blueprint. A process diagram for services where the activities are separated into two groups: customer involvement required (front office) and support behind the scenes (back office). Sometimes the service blueprint adds a third group of activities, where customer involvement may or may not be required depending on the particular circumstances (such as when a credit card is rejected for payment).

Service distribution. The variability in a service time, which can be represented by selected probability distributions that best fit the particular situation, with the exponential distribution being most commonly used.

Service rate. The average number of arrivals serviced or processed per some selected period of time. This continuous value can have a decimal component for small service rates, but it is normally rounded to whole numbers for larger rates. This value is represented by the Greek mu (μ) in waiting line equations. Some typical values are 1.2 customers per minute, 6 cars per hour, or 120 products per week.

Service time. The time required to perform a service or process. The average value is the inverse of the service rate (i.e., $1/\mu$).

Sojourn time. The total time spent in a service system. See also *waiting time*.

State-dependent rate. A rate influenced by the current state of a waiting line. See also *balking* and *reneging* for examples of factors creating a state-dependent arrival rate. Some models that have a state-dependent arrival rate are those dealing with a limited population (K) or limited queuing capacity (N).

State diagram. A graphical method showing the conditions for each state of a waiting line. Each state represents a specific number of persons or items in the queue. When the queue reaches a steady-state condition, the movements from one state to another are governed by a balance equation.

Stochastic. Having an unpredictable value because of the possibility of a wide range of possible results. As a result, stochastic variables must be represented by either discrete or continuous probability distributions in analysis methods such as queuing equations. Examples in the context of this monograph are infinite population arrival times and service times, how long a customer is willing to wait before giving up on a service line, and which of the several service lines available is selected by the next customer. See also *deterministic*.

Utilization factor. The ratio of the arrival rate λ to the service rate μ. This value is represented by the Greek rho ($\rho = \lambda/u$) in waiting line equations. This is analogous to machine capacity reduced by some percentage (cushion) to allow some time for preventive maintenance or reserve some capacity for unexpected increases in demand. This factor must be less than 1 for a single-channel waiting line situation to reach a steady state. Modifications of this factor to accommodate conditions associated with multiple servers and/or limited calling populations are indicated in this monograph by the use of appropriate subscript notation as defined in the text and in appendix B.

Waiting line cost. A measure of the estimated level of overall customer dissatisfaction. This cost can take the form of lost profit when customers are turned away by a busy situation, estimates of lost business caused by dissatisfied customers, or even work required to correct a service error. See also *balking, blocking,* and *reneging.*

Waiting time. The time spent in a waiting line or queue. The average waiting time is characterized by two values: the average time (W_q) spent in line awaiting service and the total time (W) spent in the system (waiting in line plus service time). W is often called the throughput time in manufacturing applications and the sojourn time in service applications.

WIP. Work in process for a manufacturing line. It is the number of items in a manufacturing system waiting for processing or being worked on.

APPENDIX B

Symbol Definitions

α   Represents a parameter of choice in many equations. Do not assume that α represents the same thing throughout the text.

β   Represents a parameter of choice in many equations. Do not assume that β represents the same thing throughout the text.

B   Used as a subscript to indicate performance measures related to customers or items being blocked from entering the system because of limits imposed by the maximum number of servers and places (capacity) available.

C   Represents cost in cost trade-off analysis. Various subscripts designate various types of costs: W, waiting time costs; S, server costs; B, blocking, balking, and reneging costs; L, line length costs; H, handling costs; E, equipment costs; F, facility costs; and $, finance costs.

C_x The coefficient of variation for the distribution of x. This coefficient is the ratio of the standard deviation of x to its mean, $\left(\dfrac{\sigma_x}{x}\right)$.

D   Represents a deterministic (constant) service or arrival time in Kendall notation for waiting line models.

!   The math symbol for a factorial, which is a continuous multiplication of integers from 0 to n. That is, where 0! is defined as having a value of 1 and $1 \times 2 \times 3 \times \ldots \times (n-1) \times n = n!$

E_k Represents an Erlang distribution with shape factor k in Kendall notation for waiting line models.

E(n)   The expected (mean) value of parameter n. Therefore, E(T) can represent the average time spent in a system.

G   Represents a general independent distribution in Kendall notation for waiting line models. One example is a normal distribution for service or arrival times that are relatively constant but can vary by a small percentage.

i   Used as a counter for a sequence of values in equations.

j   Used as a counter for a sequence of values in equations.

K   Represents the buffer size in Kendall notation for waiting line models (the number of places available for waiting and service when the line length is limited).

k   Shape factor for Erlang distribution. It can also be used as a counter for a sequence of values in equations.

L   The average length of a line in a service process, including the customers currently being served. That is, the total number of customers or items in the system.

L_b   The average number of customers waiting to be served in a multiple-channel service process when all the servers are busy.

λ   The average arrival rate in number per unit of time.

λ_u   The individual arrival rate per unit or customer in a limited population model.

λ'   The effective average arrival rate. For limited capacity models, $\lambda' = \lambda(1 - P_K)$; for limited population models, $\lambda' = \lambda_u(N - L)$.

L_q   The average length of the line waiting to be served.

M   Represents a Markovian distribution in Kendall notation for waiting line models. This is usually an exponential distribution for service rate and a Poisson distribution for arrival rate.

μ   The average service rate in number per unit of time.

N   The maximum number of customers or items in a finite calling population (also called a limited population).

n   The number of customers. It can also be a counter for a sequence of values in equations.

PH   Represents a phase-type distribution in Kendall notation for waiting line models with more than one phase in sequence.
One example of this is a Coxian distribution for two or more phases, where the restriction on entering the first phase first is relaxed.

P_B   The blocking probability. See also B and P_K.

P_K   The probability that the number of customers or items in the system is equal to the maximum system capacity. It is often called the blocking probability with the alternate symbol P_B.

P_n   The probability of exactly n customers in a system during the given period of time on which the associated arrival and service rates are based. In many texts, this is expressed by P(n).

P_0 The probability of no customers in the system during the given period of time on which the associated arrival and service rates are based. In other texts, this may be expressed as P(0) or even shortened to P0.

Π A math symbol for a continuous multiplication of a sequence of terms. A simplification of this function for a sequence of integers from 0 to n is called a factorial.

q Used as subscript to indicate values associated with the line awaiting service (not yet being served). Examples are line length and the time spent waiting in line.

ρ A utilization factor (λ/μ). *Note:* Some authors also use ρ as defined for ρ_s. This can be confusing when using multiple-channel queuing equations from other texts and references; be sure to check the author's use of this symbol. In this monograph, ρ always represents only λ/μ.

ρ_s The utilization factor for a multiple-channel system $(\lambda/s\mu)$.

ρ_u The utilization factor for a single unit or customer in a limited population model.

s The number of servers or channels. In some textbooks, this value is represented by c or M. (These symbols are not used here to avoid confusion with the representation for a Markovian distribution in Kendall notation for waiting line models.)

Σ The math symbol for summation of a sequence of terms.

σ The standard deviation for a normal distribution.

u A subscript used to designate a unit value. This is particularly necessary in equations for limited population models.

V_x The variance for the distribution of x. Equal to σ^2 for a normal distribution of x.

W The average total waiting time in a service process, including the time when being served.

W_b The average time spent waiting in line before being served in a multiple-channel service process when all the servers are busy.

W_q The average time spent waiting in line before being served.

APPENDIX C

Multiple-Channel Application Data

P_0, L_q, and L Tables for Multiple Server Applications								
		s = 1			s = 2			s = 3	
ρ	P_0	L_q	L	P_0	L_q	L	P_0	L_q	L
0.2	0.8000	0.0500	0.2500						
0.25	0.7500	0.0833	0.3333						
0.3	0.7000	0.1286	0.4286						
0.35	0.6500	0.1885	0.5385						
0.4	0.6000	0.2667	0.6667						
0.45	0.5500	0.3682	0.8182						
0.5	0.5000	0.5000	1.0000	0.6000	0.0333	0.5333			
0.55	0.4500	0.6722	1.2222	0.5686	0.0450	0.5950			
0.6	0.4000	0.9000	1.5000	0.5385	0.0593	0.6593			
0.65	0.3500	1.2071	1.8571	0.5094	0.0768	0.7268			
0.7	0.3000	1.6333	2.3333	0.4815	0.0977	0.7977			
0.75	0.2500	2.2500	3.0000	0.4545	0.1227	0.8727			
0.8	0.2000	3.2000	4.0000	0.4286	0.1524	0.9524			
0.82	0.1800	3.7356	4.5556	0.4184	0.1657	0.9857			
0.84	0.1600	4.4100	5.2500	0.4085	0.1799	1.0199			
0.86	0.1400	5.2829	6.1429	0.3986	0.1951	1.0551	0.4204	0.0251	0.8851
0.88	0.1200	6.4533	7.3333	0.3889	0.2113	1.0913	0.4119	0.0275	0.9075
0.9	0.1000	8.1000	9.0000	0.3793	0.2285	1.1285	0.4035	0.0300	0.9300
0.92	0.0800	10.5800	11.5000	0.3699	0.2469	1.1669	0.3952	0.0327	0.9527
0.94	0.0600	14.7267	15.6667	0.3605	0.2665	1.2065	0.3871	0.0356	0.9756
0.96	0.0400	23.0400	24.0000	0.3514	0.2874	1.2474	0.3791	0.0387	0.9987
0.98	0.0200	48.0200	49.0000	0.3423	0.3096	1.2896	0.3713	0.0420	1.0220
1	0.0000	∞	∞	0.3333	0.3333	1.3333	0.3636	0.0455	1.0455
1.1				0.2903	0.4771	1.5771	0.3273	0.0664	1.1664
1.2				0.2500	0.6750	1.8750	0.2941	0.0941	1.2941
1.3				0.2121	0.9511	2.2511	0.2638	0.1303	1.4303
1.35				0.1940	1.1299	2.4799	0.2496	0.1522	1.5022
1.4				0.1765	1.3451	2.7451	0.2360	0.1771	1.5771
1.45				0.1594	1.6067	3.0567	0.2230	0.2051	1.6551
1.5				0.1429	1.9286	3.4286	0.2105	0.2368	1.7368
1.55				0.1268	2.3311	3.8811	0.1986	0.2726	1.8226
1.6				0.1111	2.8444	4.4444	0.1872	0.3129	1.9129
1.65				0.0959	3.5163	5.1663	0.1762	0.3583	2.0083
1.7				0.0811	4.4261	6.1261	0.1657	0.4095	2.1095
1.75				0.0667	5.7167	7.4667	0.1556	0.4671	2.2171
1.8				0.0526	7.6737	9.4737	0.1460	0.5321	2.3321
1.82				0.0471	8.7676	10.5876	0.1422	0.5604	2.3804
1.84				0.0417	10.1392	11.9792	0.1385	0.5901	2.4301
1.86				0.0363	11.9076	13.7676	0.1349	0.6213	2.4813
1.88				0.0309	14.2712	16.1512	0.1313	0.6540	2.5340
1.9				0.0256	17.5872	19.4872	0.1278	0.6884	2.5884
1.92				0.0204	22.5698	24.4898	0.1244	0.7246	2.6446
1.94				0.0152	30.8857	32.8257	0.1210	0.7626	2.7026
1.96				0.0101	47.5349	49.4949	0.1176	0.8025	2.7625
1.98				0.0050	97.5175	99.4975	0.1143	0.8446	2.8246
2				0.0000	∞	∞	0.1111	0.8889	2.8889

ρ	s = 3			s = 4			s = 5		
	P_0	L_q	L	P_0	L_q	L	P_0	L_q	L
2.1	0.0957	1.1488	3.2488	0.1169	0.2204	2.3204			
2.2	0.0815	1.4909	3.6909	0.1046	0.2772	2.4772			
2.3	0.0683	1.9511	4.2511	0.0933	0.3464	2.6464			
2.35	0.0621	2.2426	4.5926	0.0881	0.3864	2.7364			
2.4	0.0562	2.5888	4.9888	0.0831	0.4306	2.8306			
2.45	0.0505	3.0047	5.4547	0.0783	0.4793	2.9293			
2.5	0.0449	3.5112	6.0112	0.0737	0.5331	3.0331			
2.55	0.0396	4.1388	6.6888	0.0693	0.5925	3.1425			
2.6	0.0345	4.9328	7.5328	0.0651	0.6582	3.2582			
2.65	0.0296	5.9647	8.6147	0.0612	0.7309	3.3809			
2.7	0.0249	7.3535	10.0535	0.0573	0.8115	3.5115			
2.75	0.0204	9.3136	12.0636	0.0537	0.9008	3.6508			
2.8	0.0160	12.2735	15.0735	0.0502	1.0002	3.8002	0.0581	0.2412	3.0412
2.82	0.0143	13.9240	16.7440	0.0489	1.0430	3.8630	0.0569	0.2508	3.0708
2.84	0.0126	15.9912	18.8312	0.0475	1.0878	3.9278	0.0557	0.2608	3.1008
2.86	0.0109	18.6536	21.5136	0.0462	1.1345	3.9945	0.0545	0.2712	3.1312
2.88	0.0093	22.2089	25.0889	0.0450	1.1834	4.0634	0.0533	0.2819	3.1619
2.9	0.0077	27.1927	30.0927	0.0437	1.2345	4.1345	0.0521	0.2929	3.1929
2.92	0.0061	34.6764	37.5964	0.0425	1.2879	4.2079	0.0510	0.3044	3.2244
2.94	0.0045	47.1601	50.1001	0.0412	1.3439	4.2839	0.0499	0.3162	3.2562
2.96	0.0030	72.1438	75.1038	0.0401	1.4025	4.3625	0.0488	0.3284	3.2884
2.98	0.0015	147.1275	150.1075	0.0389	1.4639	4.4439	0.0477	0.3411	3.3211
3	0.0000	∞	∞	0.0377	1.5283	4.5283	0.0466	0.3542	3.3542
3.1				0.0323	1.9019	5.0019	0.0417	0.4269	3.5269
3.2				0.0273	2.3857	5.5857	0.0372	0.5130	3.7130
3.3				0.0227	3.0273	6.3273	0.0330	0.6152	3.9152
3.4				0.0186	3.9061	7.3061	0.0293	0.7367	4.1367
3.5				0.0148	5.1650	8.6650	0.0259	0.8816	4.3816
3.6				0.0113	7.0898	10.6898	0.0228	1.0553	4.6553
3.7				0.0081	10.3471	14.0471	0.0200	1.2646	4.9646
3.75				0.0066	12.9754	16.7254	0.0187	1.3854	5.1354
3.8				0.0051	16.9370	20.7370	0.0174	1.5187	5.3187
3.85				0.0038	23.5650	27.4150	0.0162	1.6663	5.5163
3.9				0.0025	36.8595	40.7595	0.0151	1.8302	5.7302
3.92				0.0019	46.8439	50.7639	0.0147	1.9008	5.8208
3.94				0.0014	63.4949	67.4349	0.0142	1.9745	5.9145
3.96				0.0010	96.8126	100.7726	0.0138	2.0516	6.0116
3.98				0.0005	196.7969	200.7769	0.0134	2.1321	6.1121
4				0.0000	∞	∞	0.0130	2.2165	6.2165
4.1							0.0111	2.7029	6.8029
4.2							0.0093	3.3273	7.5273
4.3							0.0077	4.1493	8.4493
4.4							0.0063	5.2682	9.6682
4.5							0.0050	6.8624	11.3624
4.6							0.0038	9.2893	13.8893
4.7							0.0027	13.3821	18.0821
4.75							0.0022	16.6782	21.4282
4.8							0.0017	21.6408	26.4408
4.85							0.0012	29.9366	34.7866
4.9							0.0008	46.5655	51.4655
4.95							0.0004	96.5276	101.4776
5							0.0000	∞	∞

ρ	s = 6			s = 7			s = 8		
	P_0	L_q	L	P_0	L_q	L	P_0	L_q	L
3.5	0.0290	0.2485	3.7485						
3.6	0.0260	0.2948	3.8948						
3.7	0.0233	0.3488	4.0488						
3.75	0.0221	0.3790	4.1290						
3.8	0.0209	0.4116	4.2116						
3.85	0.0198	0.4467	4.2967						
3.9	0.0187	0.4846	4.3846						
3.92	0.0183	0.5006	4.4206						
3.94	0.0179	0.5170	4.4570						
3.96	0.0175	0.5340	4.4940						
3.98	0.0171	0.5515	4.5315						
4	0.0167	0.5695	4.5695						
4.1	0.0149	0.6685	4.7685						
4.2	0.0132	0.7839	4.9839	0.0144	0.2476	4.4476			
4.3	0.0117	0.9191	5.2191	0.0130	0.2890	4.5890			
4.4	0.0104	1.0778	5.4778	0.0117	0.3365	4.7365			
4.5	0.0091	1.2650	5.7650	0.0105	0.3910	4.8910			
4.6	0.0080	1.4869	6.0869	0.0094	0.4535	5.0535			
4.7	0.0070	1.7520	6.4520	0.0084	0.5251	5.2251			
4.75	0.0065	1.9039	6.6539	0.0079	0.5648	5.3148			
4.8	0.0061	2.0711	6.8711	0.0075	0.6073	5.4073			
4.85	0.0057	2.2554	7.1054	0.0071	0.6529	5.5029			
4.9	0.0053	2.4593	7.3593	0.0067	0.7017	5.6017	0.0072	0.2418	5.1418
4.95	0.0049	2.6856	7.6356	0.0063	0.7541	5.7041	0.0068	0.2597	5.2097
5	0.0045	2.9376	7.9376	0.0060	0.8104	5.8104	0.0065	0.2788	5.2788
5.1	0.0038	3.5363	8.6363	0.0053	0.9357	6.0357	0.0058	0.3207	5.4207
5.2	0.0032	4.3009	9.5009	0.0047	1.0805	6.2805	0.0052	0.3683	5.5683
5.3	0.0027	5.3028	10.6028	0.0042	1.2486	6.5486	0.0047	0.4222	5.7222
5.4	0.0021	6.6611	12.0611	0.0037	1.4444	6.8444	0.0042	0.4833	5.8833
5.5	0.0017	8.5902	14.0902	0.0032	1.6736	7.1736	0.0038	0.5527	6.0527
5.6	0.0013	11.5185	17.1185	0.0028	1.9438	7.5438	0.0034	0.6314	6.2314
5.7	0.0009	16.4462	22.1462	0.0025	2.2643	7.9643	0.0030	0.7208	6.4208
5.75	0.0007	20.4098	26.1598	0.0023	2.4474	8.1974	0.0029	0.7701	6.5201
5.8	0.0006	26.3732	32.1732	0.0021	2.6482	8.4482	0.0027	0.8226	6.6226
5.85	0.0004	36.3365	42.1865	0.0020	2.8692	8.7192	0.0026	0.8786	6.7286
5.9	0.0003	56.2996	62.1996	0.0018	3.1130	9.0130	0.0024	0.9385	6.8385
5.95	0.0001	116.2625	122.2125	0.0017	3.3829	9.3329	0.0023	1.0025	6.9525
6	0.0000	∞	∞	0.0016	3.6830	9.6830	0.0021	1.0709	7.0709
6.1				0.0013	4.3937	10.4937	0.0019	1.2226	7.3226
6.2				0.0011	5.2981	11.4981	0.0017	1.3968	7.5968
6.3				0.0009	6.4796	12.7796	0.0015	1.5977	7.8977
6.4				0.0007	8.0771	14.4771	0.0013	1.8306	8.2306
6.5				0.0006	10.3406	16.8406	0.0012	2.1019	8.6019
6.6				0.0004	13.7701	20.3701	0.0010	2.4200	9.0200
6.7				0.0003	19.5323	26.2323	0.0009	2.7960	9.4960
6.75				0.0003	24.1631	30.9131	0.0008	3.0101	9.7601
6.8				0.0002	31.1272	37.9272	0.0008	3.2446	10.0446
6.85				0.0001	42.7577	49.6077	0.0007	3.5020	10.3520
6.9				0.0001	66.0548	72.9548	0.0007	3.7856	10.6856
6.95				0.0000	136.0184	142.9684	0.0006	4.0992	11.0492
7				0.0000	∞	∞	0.0006	4.4472	11.4472

ρ	s = 8			s = 9			s = 10		
	P_0	L_q	L	P_0	L_q	L	P_0	L_q	L
5.6	0.0034	0.6314	6.2314	0.0036	0.2332	5.8332			
5.7	0.0030	0.7208	6.4208	0.0032	0.2662	5.9662			
5.75	0.0029	0.7701	6.5201	0.0031	0.2842	6.0342			
5.8	0.0027	0.8226	6.6226	0.0029	0.3033	6.1033			
5.85	0.0026	0.8786	6.7286	0.0028	0.3236	6.1736			
5.9	0.0024	0.9385	6.8385	0.0026	0.3451	6.2451			
5.95	0.0023	1.0025	6.9525	0.0025	0.3678	6.3178			
6	0.0021	1.0709	7.0709	0.0024	0.3920	6.3920			
6.1	0.0019	1.2226	7.3226	0.0021	0.4447	6.5447			
6.2	0.0017	1.3968	7.5968	0.0019	0.5039	6.7039			
6.3	0.0015	1.5977	7.8977	0.0017	0.5705	6.8705	0.0018	0.2230	6.5230
6.4	0.0013	1.8306	8.2306	0.0015	0.6455	7.0455	0.0016	0.2525	6.6525
6.5	0.0012	2.1019	8.6019	0.0014	0.7298	7.2298	0.0015	0.2855	6.7855
6.6	0.0010	2.4200	9.0200	0.0012	0.8249	7.4249	0.0013	0.3223	6.9223
6.7	0.0009	2.7960	9.4960	0.0011	0.9323	7.6323	0.0012	0.3634	7.0634
6.75	0.0008	3.0101	9.7601	0.0010	0.9911	7.7411	0.0011	0.3857	7.1357
6.8	0.0008	3.2446	10.0446	0.0010	1.0536	7.8536	0.0011	0.4092	7.2092
6.85	0.0007	3.5020	10.3520	0.0009	1.1202	7.9702	0.0010	0.4341	7.2841
6.9	0.0007	3.7856	10.6856	0.0009	1.1911	8.0911	0.0010	0.4603	7.3603
6.95	0.0006	4.0992	11.0492	0.0008	1.2667	8.2167	0.0009	0.4881	7.4381
7	0.0006	4.4472	11.4472	0.0008	1.3473	8.3473	0.0009	0.5174	7.5174
7.1	0.0005	5.2697	12.3697	0.0007	1.5253	8.6253	0.0008	0.5810	7.6810
7.2	0.0004	6.3138	13.5138	0.0006	1.7289	8.9289	0.0007	0.6521	7.8521
7.3	0.0003	7.6747	14.9747	0.0005	1.9627	9.2627	0.0006	0.7315	8.0315
7.4	0.0003	9.5111	16.9111	0.0005	2.2325	9.6325	0.0006	0.8204	8.2204
7.5	0.0002	12.1088	19.6088	0.0004	2.5457	10.0457	0.0005	0.9198	8.4198
7.6	0.0002	16.0392	23.6392	0.0004	2.9118	10.5118	0.0004	1.0314	8.6314
7.7	0.0001	22.6357	30.3357	0.0003	3.3432	11.0432	0.0004	1.1566	8.8566
7.75	0.0001	27.9337	35.6837	0.0003	3.5883	11.3383	0.0004	1.2250	8.9750
7.8	0.0001	35.8982	43.6982	0.0003	3.8563	11.6563	0.0004	1.2976	9.0976
7.85	0.0000	49.1960	57.0460	0.0002	4.1502	12.0002	0.0003	1.3747	9.2247
7.9	0.0000	75.8269	83.7269	0.0002	4.4736	12.3736	0.0003	1.4567	9.3567
7.95	0.0000	155.7910	163.7410	0.0002	4.8307	12.7807	0.0003	1.5439	9.4939
8	0.0000	∞	∞	0.0002	5.2266	13.2266	0.0003	1.6367	9.6367
8.1				0.0002	6.1608	14.2608	0.0002	1.8411	9.9411
8.2				0.0001	7.3444	15.5444	0.0002	2.0740	10.2740
8.3				0.0001	8.8845	17.1845	0.0002	2.3406	10.6406
8.4				0.0001	10.9597	19.3597	0.0002	2.6474	11.0474
8.5				0.0001	13.8914	22.3914	0.0001	3.0025	11.5025
8.6				0.0001	18.3226	26.9226	0.0001	3.4166	12.0166
8.7				0.0000	25.7532	34.4532	0.0001	3.9032	12.6032
8.75				0.0000	31.7183	40.4683	0.0001	4.1792	12.9292
8.8				0.0000	40.6832	49.4832	0.0001	4.4807	13.2807
8.85				0.0000	55.6481	64.4981	0.0001	4.8111	13.6611
8.9				0.0000	85.6127	94.5127	0.0001	5.1742	14.0742
8.95				0.0000	175.5773	184.5273	0.0001	5.5748	14.5248
9				0.0000	∞	∞	0.0001	6.0186	15.0186
9.1							0.0001	7.0644	16.1644
9.2							0.0000	8.3873	17.5873
9.3							0.0000	10.1066	19.4066
9.4							0.0000	12.4204	21.8204
9.5							0.0000	15.6861	25.1861
9.6							0.0000	20.6179	30.2179
9.7							0.0000	28.8825	38.5825
9.75							0.0000	35.5146	45.2646
9.8							0.0000	45.4799	55.2799
9.85							0.0000	62.1117	71.9617
9.9							0.0000	95.4101	105.3101
9.95							0.0000	195.3750	205.3250
10							0.0000	∞	∞

The following printouts are from Example 5.1 for the N = 10, s = 3 calculations. This page shows the output from Excel, and the following pages show the intermediate calculations and their respective Excel formulas. Values for P_0, L_q, and L for all of the N and s sets are recorded in the table from previous runs by pasting just the results into the table.

P₀, Lq, and L Tables for Multiple Server Applications with Finite Populations

Population Size (N) =	10	$N! =$	3628800	
Servers (s) =	3	$s! =$	6	
$\rho_u =$	0.016	$P_0 =$	0.853220136	
		$L_q =$	1.66999E-05	
		$L =$	0.157496752	

		s = 1			s = 2			s = 3		
N	ρ_u	P_0	L_q	L	P_0	L_q	L	P_0	L_q	L
10	0.016	0.842919	0.025346	0.182427	0.8530	0.0007	0.1582	0.8532	0.0000	0.1575
25	0.016	0.6098	0.2254	0.6155	0.6694	0.0138	0.4073	0.6723	0.0009	0.3946
50	0.016	0.242301	1.8861	2.6438	0.4338	0.1313	0.9166	0.4504	0.0158	0.8030
λ				0.0393			0.0394			0.0394
λ				0.0975			0.0984			0.0984
λ				0.1894			0.1963			0.1968
W_q			0.6454			0.0179			0.0005	
W_q			2.3106			0.1408			0.0096	
W_q			9.9570			0.6686			0.0803	
W				4.6454			4.0179			4.0004
W				6.3106			4.1408			4.0096
W				13.9570			4.6686			4.0803

P₀, L_q, and L Tables for Multiple Server Applications with Finite Populations

		Population Size (N) = 10
		Servers (s) = 3
		p_e = 0.016

Right-side formulas:

- N! = =FACT(N)
- s! = =FACT(s)
- P₀ = =1/(H17+I17)
- L_q = =I17
- L = =SUM(K6:K8)+T6+s*(1-SUM(J6:J8))

n	P_e	s=1 P₀	s=1 L_q	s=1 L	s=2 P₀	s=2 L_q	s=2 L	s=3 P₀	s=3 L_q	s=3 L
10	0.016	0.342918839556663	0.0253463118481259	0.182427472291463	0.8530235105565085	0.000704709106987002	0.1581739262636404	0.8532201363163182	0.0000190391482646	0.157496751897711
25	0.016	0.609848403559646	0.225373626037527	0.615552522477881	0.669382203723071	0.0138478473959615	0.4073305584660592	0.6722848794113815	0.0009403024787833016	0.394626281967306
50	0.016	0.2423008361115135	1.88610309331109	2.643802257195966	0.433809112583166	0.131260217286951	0.916594702054085	0.45035154422874	0.015806578538042	0.802959230844529
λ				=0.004*(N12-R12)			=0.004*(N12-U12)			=0.004*(N12-X12)
λ				=0.004*(N13-R13)			=0.004*(N13-U13)			=0.004*(N13-X13)
λ				=0.004*(N14-R14)			=0.004*(N14-U14)			=0.004*(N14-X14)
W_q			=Q12/R16			=T12/U16			=W12/X16	
W_q			=Q13/R17			=T13/U17			=W13/X17	
W_q			=Q14/R18			=T14/U18			=W14/X18	
W				=R12/R16			=U12/U16			=X12/X16
W				=R13/R17			=U13/U17			=X13/X17
W				=R14/R18			=U14/U18			=X14/X18

n	n!	(N-n)!	N!/(N-n)!	s^{n-s}	$(\rho_u)^n$	P_0 Term 1	P_0 Term 2	P_n	nP_n	$(n-s)P_n$
0	1	3628800	1	0.037037	1	1		0.85322	0	-2.55966
1	1	362880	10	0.111111	0.016	0.16		0.136515	0.136515	-0.27303
2	2	40320	90	0.333333	0.000256	0.01152		0.009829	0.019658	-0.009829
3	6	5040	720	1	4.1E-06		0.000492	0.000419	0.001258	0
4	24	720	5040	3	6.55E-08		1.84E-05	1.57E-05	6.26E-05	1.57E-05
5	120	120	30240	9	1.05E-09		5.87E-07	5.01E-07	2.51E-06	1E-06
6	720	24	151200	27	1.68E-11		1.57E-08	1.34E-08	8.02E-08	4.01E-08
7	5040	6	604800	81	2.68E-13		3.34E-10	2.85E-10	2E-09	1.14E-09
8	40320	2	1814400	243	4.29E-15		5.34E-12	4.56E-12	3.65E-11	2.28E-11
9	362880	1	3628800	729	6.87E-17		5.7E-14	4.86E-14	4.38E-13	2.92E-13
10	3628800	1	3628800	2187	1.1E-18		3.04E-16	2.59E-16	2.59E-15	1.82E-15
Summations -->						1.17152	0.00051	1		1.67E-05

	A	B	C	D	E	F	G	H	I	J	K
5	n	$n!$	$(N-n)!$	$N!/(N-n)!$	s^{n-s}	$(\rho_0)^n$	P_0 Term 1	P_0 Term 2	P_n	nP_n	$(n-s)*P_n$
6	0	=FACT(A6)	=FACT(N-A6)	=$S$3/C6	=s^(A6-s)	=SQ$5^A6	=F6*D6/B6		=S5	=A6*I6	=(A6-s)*I6
7	1	=FACT(A7)	=FACT(N-A7)	=$S$3/C7	=s^(A7-s)	=SQ$5	=F7*D7/B7		=$S$5*G7	=A7*I7	=(A7-s)*I7
8	2	=FACT(A8)	=FACT(N-A8)	=$S$3/C8	=s^(A8-s)	=SQ$5^A8	=F8*D8/B8		=$S$5*G8	=A8*I8	=(A8-s)*I8
9	3	=FACT(A9)	=FACT(N-A9)	=$S$3/C9	=s^(A9-s)	=SQ$5^A9		=D9*F9/(E9*S$S$4)	=$S$5*H9	=A9*I9	=(A9-s)*I9
10	4	=FACT(A10)	=FACT(N-A10)	=$S$3/C10	=s^(A10-s)	=SQ$5^A10		=D10*F10/(E10*S$S$4)	=$S$5*H10	=A10*I10	=(A10-s)*I10
11	5	=FACT(A11)	=FACT(N-A11)	=$S$3/C11	=s^(A11-s)	=SQ$5^A11		=D11*F11/(E11*S$S$4)	=$S$5*H11	=A11*I11	=(A11-s)*I11
12	6	=FACT(A12)	=FACT(N-A12)	=$S$3/C12	=s^(A12-s)	=SQ$5^A12		=D12*F12/(E12*S$S$4)	=$S$5*H12	=A12*I12	=(A12-s)*I12
13	7	=FACT(A13)	=FACT(N-A13)	=$S$3/C13	=s^(A13-s)	=SQ$5^A13		=D13*F13/(E13*S$S$4)	=$S$5*H13	=A13*I13	=(A13-s)*I13
14	8	=FACT(A14)	=FACT(N-A14)	=$S$3/C14	=s^(A14-s)	=SQ$5^A14		=D14*F14/(E14*S$S$4)	=$S$5*H14	=A14*I14	=(A14-s)*I14
15	9	=FACT(A15)	=FACT(N-A15)	=$S$3/C15	=s^(A15-s)	=SQ$5^A15		=D15*F15/(E15*S$S$4)	=$S$5*H15	=A15*I15	=(A15-s)*I15
16	10	=FACT(A16)	=FACT(N-A16)	=$S$3/C16	=s^(A16-s)	=SQ$5^A16		=D16*F16/(E16*S$S$4)	=$S$5*H16	=A16*I16	=(A16-s)*I16
17					Summations -- >		=SUM(G6:G16)	=SUM(H6:H16)	=SUM(I6:I16)		=SUM(K9:K16)

Learning Curve Tables (multiply all times by same constant to make repetition time 1 = actual value for first time)

Repetition Number	70%, b = -0.514573		75%, b = -0.415037		80%, b = -0.321928		85%, b = -0.234465		90%, b = -0.152003	
	Repetition Time	Total Time Elapsed	Repetition Time	Total Time Elapsed	Repetition Time	Total Time Elapsed	Repetition Time	Total Time Elapsed	Repetition Time	Total Time Elapsed
1	1.0000	1.0000	1.0000	1.0000	1.0000	1.0000	1.0000	1.0000	1.0000	1.0000
2	0.7000	1.7000	0.7500	1.7500	0.8000	1.8000	0.8500	1.8500	0.9000	1.9000
3	0.5682	2.2682	0.6338	2.3838	0.7021	2.5021	0.7729	2.6229	0.8462	2.7462
4	0.4900	2.7582	0.5625	2.9463	0.6400	3.1421	0.7225	3.3454	0.8100	3.5562
5	0.4368	3.1950	0.5127	3.4591	0.5956	3.7377	0.6857	4.0311	0.7830	4.3392
6	0.3977	3.5928	0.4754	3.9345	0.5617	4.2994	0.6570	4.6881	0.7616	5.1008
7	0.3674	3.9602	0.4459	4.3804	0.5345	4.8339	0.6337	5.3217	0.7439	5.8447
8	0.3430	4.3032	0.4219	4.8023	0.5120	5.3459	0.6141	5.9358	0.7290	6.5737
9	0.3228	4.6260	0.4017	5.2040	0.4929	5.8389	0.5974	6.5332	0.7161	7.2898
10	0.3058	4.9318	0.3846	5.5886	0.4765	6.3154	0.5828	7.1161	0.7047	7.9945
11	0.2912	5.2229	0.3696	5.9582	0.4621	6.7775	0.5699	7.6860	0.6946	8.6890
12	0.2784	5.5013	0.3565	6.3147	0.4493	7.2268	0.5584	8.2444	0.6854	9.3745
13	0.2672	5.7685	0.3449	6.6596	0.4379	7.6647	0.5480	8.7925	0.6771	10.0516
14	0.2572	6.0257	0.3344	6.9941	0.4276	8.0923	0.5386	9.3311	0.6696	10.7212
15	0.2482	6.2739	0.3250	7.3191	0.4182	8.5105	0.5300	9.8611	0.6626	11.3837
16	0.2401	6.5140	0.3164	7.6355	0.4096	8.9201	0.5220	10.3831	0.6561	12.0398
17	0.2327	6.7467	0.3085	7.9440	0.4017	9.3218	0.5146	10.8977	0.6501	12.6899
18	0.2260	6.9727	0.3013	8.2453	0.3944	9.7162	0.5078	11.4055	0.6445	13.3344
19	0.2198	7.1925	0.2946	8.5399	0.3876	10.1037	0.5014	11.9069	0.6392	13.9735
20	0.2141	7.4065	0.2884	8.8284	0.3812	10.4849	0.4954	12.4023	0.6342	14.6078
21	0.2087	7.6153	0.2826	9.1110	0.3753	10.8602	0.4898	12.8920	0.6295	15.2373
22	0.2038	7.8191	0.2772	9.3882	0.3697	11.2299	0.4844	13.3765	0.6251	15.8624
23	0.1992	8.0183	0.2722	9.6604	0.3644	11.5943	0.4794	13.8559	0.6209	16.4833
24	0.1949	8.2132	0.2674	9.9278	0.3595	11.9538	0.4747	14.3306	0.6169	17.1002
25	0.1908	8.4040	0.2629	10.1907	0.3548	12.3086	0.4701	14.8007	0.6131	17.7132
26	0.1870	8.5910	0.2587	10.4494	0.3503	12.6589	0.4658	15.2666	0.6094	18.3227
27	0.1834	8.7745	0.2546	10.7040	0.3461	13.0050	0.4617	15.7283	0.6059	18.9286
28	0.1800	8.9545	0.2508	10.9548	0.3421	13.3471	0.4578	16.1861	0.6026	19.5312
29	0.1768	9.1313	0.2472	11.2020	0.3382	13.6853	0.4541	16.6402	0.5994	20.1306
30	0.1737	9.3050	0.2437	11.4458	0.3346	14.0199	0.4505	17.0907	0.5963	20.7269
31	0.1708	9.4759	0.2405	11.6862	0.3310	14.3509	0.4470	17.5377	0.5933	21.3202
32	0.1681	9.6439	0.2373	11.9235	0.3277	14.6786	0.4437	17.9814	0.5905	21.9107
33	0.1654	9.8094	0.2343	12.1578	0.3245	15.0031	0.4405	18.4219	0.5877	22.4985
34	0.1629	9.9723	0.2314	12.3892	0.3213	15.3244	0.4374	18.8594	0.5851	23.0835
35	0.1605	10.1328	0.2286	12.6179	0.3184	15.6428	0.4345	19.2938	0.5825	23.6660
36	0.1582	10.2910	0.2260	12.8439	0.3155	15.9583	0.4316	19.7255	0.5800	24.2461
37	0.1560	10.4469	0.2234	13.0673	0.3127	16.2710	0.4289	20.1543	0.5776	24.8237
38	0.1538	10.6008	0.2210	13.2883	0.3100	16.5810	0.4262	20.5805	0.5753	25.3989
39	0.1518	10.7526	0.2186	13.5069	0.3075	16.8885	0.4236	21.0041	0.5730	25.9719
40	0.1498	10.9024	0.2163	13.7232	0.3050	17.1935	0.4211	21.4252	0.5708	26.5427
41	0.1479	11.0504	0.2141	13.9373	0.3026	17.4960	0.4187	21.8438	0.5687	27.1114
42	0.1461	11.1965	0.2120	14.1493	0.3002	17.7962	0.4163	22.2601	0.5666	27.6780
43	0.1444	11.3409	0.2099	14.3592	0.2979	18.0942	0.4140	22.6741	0.5646	28.2425
44	0.1427	11.4835	0.2079	14.5671	0.2958	18.3899	0.4118	23.0859	0.5626	28.8051
45	0.1410	11.6246	0.2060	14.7731	0.2936	18.6835	0.4096	23.4955	0.5607	29.3658
46	0.1394	11.7640	0.2041	14.9772	0.2915	18.9751	0.4075	23.9031	0.5588	29.9246
47	0.1379	11.9019	0.2023	15.1795	0.2895	19.2646	0.4055	24.3085	0.5570	30.4815
48	0.1364	12.0383	0.2006	15.3801	0.2876	19.5522	0.4035	24.7120	0.5552	31.0367
49	0.1350	12.1733	0.1988	15.5789	0.2857	19.8379	0.4015	25.1135	0.5535	31.5902
50	0.1336	12.3069	0.1972	15.7761	0.2838	20.1217	0.3996	25.5131	0.5518	32.1420

Repetition Number	70%, b = -0.514573		75%, b = -0.415037		80%, b = -0.321928		85%, b = -0.234465		90%, b = -0.152003	
	Repetition Time	Total Time Elapsed	Repetition Time	Total Time Elapsed	Repetition Time	Total Time Elapsed	Repetition Time	Total Time Elapsed	Repetition Time	Total Time Elapsed
51	0.1322	12.4391	0.1956	15.9717	0.2820	20.4037	0.3978	25.9109	0.5501	32.6921
52	0.1309	12.5700	0.1940	16.1657	0.2803	20.6840	0.3960	26.3069	0.5485	33.2405
53	0.1296	12.6997	0.1925	16.3581	0.2786	20.9626	0.3942	26.7011	0.5469	33.7874
54	0.1284	12.8281	0.1910	16.5491	0.2769	21.2394	0.3925	27.0935	0.5453	34.3328
55	0.1272	12.9553	0.1895	16.7387	0.2753	21.5147	0.3908	27.4843	0.5438	34.8766
56	0.1260	13.0813	0.1881	16.9268	0.2737	21.7884	0.3891	27.8735	0.5423	35.4190
57	0.1249	13.2062	0.1867	17.1135	0.2721	22.0605	0.3875	28.2610	0.5409	35.9598
58	0.1238	13.3299	0.1854	17.2989	0.2706	22.3310	0.3860	28.6470	0.5395	36.4993
59	0.1227	13.4526	0.1841	17.4830	0.2691	22.6001	0.3844	29.0314	0.5381	37.0373
60	0.1216	13.5742	0.1828	17.6658	0.2676	22.8678	0.3829	29.4143	0.5367	37.5740
61	0.1206	13.6948	0.1816	17.8474	0.2662	23.1340	0.3814	29.7957	0.5353	38.1094
62	0.1196	13.8144	0.1803	18.0277	0.2648	23.3989	0.3800	30.1757	0.5340	38.6434
63	0.1186	13.9330	0.1791	18.2069	0.2635	23.6623	0.3785	30.5542	0.5327	39.1761
64	0.1176	14.0506	0.1780	18.3849	0.2621	23.9245	0.3771	30.9314	0.5314	39.7075
65	0.1167	14.1674	0.1768	18.5617	0.2608	24.1853	0.3758	31.3071	0.5302	40.2377
66	0.1158	14.2832	0.1757	18.7374	0.2596	24.4449	0.3744	31.6816	0.5290	40.7667
67	0.1149	14.3981	0.1746	18.9120	0.2583	24.7032	0.3731	32.0547	0.5278	41.2944
68	0.1140	14.5121	0.1736	19.0856	0.2571	24.9603	0.3718	32.4265	0.5266	41.8210
69	0.1132	14.6253	0.1725	19.2581	0.2559	25.2161	0.3706	32.7971	0.5254	42.3464
70	0.1123	14.7376	0.1715	19.4296	0.2547	25.4708	0.3693	33.1664	0.5243	42.8706
71	0.1115	14.8492	0.1705	19.6001	0.2535	25.7243	0.3681	33.5345	0.5231	43.3938
72	0.1107	14.9599	0.1695	19.7695	0.2524	25.9767	0.3669	33.9014	0.5220	43.9158
73	0.1099	15.0698	0.1685	19.9381	0.2513	26.2280	0.3657	34.2670	0.5209	44.4367
74	0.1092	15.1790	0.1676	20.1056	0.2502	26.4782	0.3645	34.6316	0.5198	44.9565
75	0.1084	15.2875	0.1666	20.2723	0.2491	26.7273	0.3634	34.9950	0.5188	45.4753
76	0.1077	15.3951	0.1657	20.4380	0.2480	26.9753	0.3623	35.3572	0.5177	45.9931
77	0.1070	15.5021	0.1648	20.6028	0.2470	27.2223	0.3611	35.7184	0.5167	46.5098
78	0.1063	15.6084	0.1639	20.7668	0.2460	27.4683	0.3601	36.0784	0.5157	47.0255
79	0.1056	15.7139	0.1631	20.9299	0.2450	27.7132	0.3590	36.4374	0.5147	47.5402
80	0.1049	15.8188	0.1622	21.0921	0.2440	27.9572	0.3579	36.7953	0.5137	48.0539
81	0.1042	15.9231	0.1614	21.2535	0.2430	28.2002	0.3569	37.1522	0.5127	48.5666
82	0.1036	16.0266	0.1606	21.4141	0.2420	28.4423	0.3559	37.5081	0.5118	49.0784
83	0.1029	16.1295	0.1598	21.5739	0.2411	28.6834	0.3548	37.8629	0.5109	49.5893
84	0.1023	16.2318	0.1590	21.7328	0.2402	28.9235	0.3539	38.2168	0.5099	50.0992
85	0.1017	16.3335	0.1582	21.8911	0.2393	29.1628	0.3529	38.5696	0.5090	50.6082
86	0.1011	16.4345	0.1574	22.0485	0.2384	29.4011	0.3519	38.9216	0.5081	51.1163
87	0.1005	16.5350	0.1567	22.2052	0.2375	29.6386	0.3510	39.2725	0.5072	51.6235
88	0.0999	16.6349	0.1559	22.3611	0.2366	29.8752	0.3500	39.6225	0.5063	52.1298
89	0.0993	16.7341	0.1552	22.5163	0.2357	30.1110	0.3491	39.9716	0.5055	52.6353
90	0.0987	16.8329	0.1545	22.6708	0.2349	30.3459	0.3482	40.3198	0.5046	53.1399
91	0.0982	16.9310	0.1538	22.8246	0.2341	30.5799	0.3473	40.6671	0.5038	53.6437
92	0.0976	17.0286	0.1531	22.9777	0.2332	30.8132	0.3464	41.0134	0.5029	54.1466
93	0.0971	17.1257	0.1524	23.1301	0.2324	31.0456	0.3455	41.3590	0.5021	54.6487
94	0.0965	17.2222	0.1517	23.2819	0.2316	31.2772	0.3446	41.7036	0.5013	55.1500
95	0.0960	17.3182	0.1511	23.4329	0.2308	31.5081	0.3438	42.0474	0.5005	55.6504
96	0.0955	17.4137	0.1504	23.5833	0.2301	31.7381	0.3429	42.3903	0.4997	56.1501
97	0.0950	17.5087	0.1498	23.7331	0.2293	31.9674	0.3421	42.7325	0.4989	56.6490
98	0.0945	17.6032	0.1491	23.8822	0.2285	32.1960	0.3413	43.0737	0.4981	57.1471
99	0.0940	17.6972	0.1485	24.0307	0.2278	32.4238	0.3405	43.4142	0.4973	57.6445
100	0.0935	17.7907	0.1479	24.1786	0.2271	32.6508	0.3397	43.7539	0.4966	58.1410

APPENDIX D

Simulation Information

This appendix serves as a reference for readers who are interested in developing their own simulation models using Excel. Figure D.1 shows the Excel expressions used for the M/M/1 simulation module described in Figures 7.6 and 7.7. Additional expressions for using random numbers to generate input values for simulation are provided along with some general tips for using Excel. A description of useful Excel functions and capabilities for simulation applications completes this appendix.

Basic simulation module set up for an M/M/1 model. Note the necessary differences in the equations for the first three customers or items. To help identify what the cell addresses in the formulas are referring to, the cell address for the "Arrival Time" label is C11. See Figure D.1.

Inverse probability distributions expressions for simulating operating values using random number (RN) inputs. Some of these distributions can be used in simulating failure probabilities for maintenance service applications or for distributing arrivals.

Exponential distribution. $t = -(1/(\lambda \text{ or } \mu) \times \ln(RN)$
Uniform distribution. (min value = a, max value = b): $t = a + RN(b - a)$; for an equivalent Excel function, use RANDBETWEEN(a,b)
Normal distribution.[1] $t = t_{avg} + \sigma \left[\sum_{i=1}^{12} RN_i - 6 \right]$ for an equivalent Excel function, use NORM.INV(RN,mean,sigma)
Beta distribution. Use Excel's BETA.INV(RN,α,β,A,B) function.
Gamma distribution (often used instead of Erlang's distribution). Use Excel's GAMMA.INV(RN,α,β) function.
Log normal distribution. Use Excel's LOGNORM.INV(RN,mean,standard_dev) function.

Basic Single-Channel, Single-Phase Model M/M/1 Simulation

Conditions:

Clock starts at zero.

No customers (units) are waiting in line at the beginning.

Arrival and service times are exponentially distributed.

Times are in minutes.

Number in line awaiting service includes the latest customer (unit) to arrive.

Slack time is time server waits after previous customer (unit) departs until current customer (unit) arrives.

Inputs:

Average Arrival Rate =

Average Service Rate =

Unit	Arrival Time	Service Starts	Service Ends	Wait in Line W_q	Time in System W	Service Time	Number in System L	Slack Time
1	=-(1/$I$4)*LN(RAND())	=B12	=C12-(1/$I$5)*LN(RAND())	=C12-B12	=D12-B12	=D12-C12	0	=B12
2	=-(1/$I$4)*LN(RAND())+B12	=IF(D12>B13,D12,B13)	=C13-(1/$I$5)*LN(RAND())	=C13-B13	=D13-B13	=D13-C13	=COUNTIF($D$12:D13,">"&B13)	=C13-D12
3	=-(1/$I$4)*LN(RAND())+B13	=IF(D13>B14,D13,B14)	=C14-(1/$I$5)*LN(RAND())	=C14-B14	=D14-B14	=D14-C14	=COUNTIF($D$12:D14,">"&B14)	=C14-D13
4	=-(1/$I$4)*LN(RAND())+B14	=IF(D14>B15,D14,B15)	=C15-(1/$I$5)*LN(RAND())	=C15-B15	=D15-B15	=D15-C15	=COUNTIF($D$12:D15,">"&B15)	=C15-D14
5	=-(1/$I$4)*LN(RAND())+B15	=IF(D15>B16,D15,B16)	=C16-(1/$I$5)*LN(RAND())	=C16-B16	=D16-B16	=D16-C16	=COUNTIF($D$12:D16,">"&B16)	=C16-D15
6	=-(1/$I$4)*LN(RAND())+B16	=IF(D16>B17,D16,B17)	=C17-(1/$I$5)*LN(RAND())	=C17-B17	=D17-B17	=D17-C17	=COUNTIF($D$12:D17,">"&B17)	=C17-D16
7	=-(1/$I$4)*LN(RAND())+B17	=IF(D17>B18,D17,B18)	=C18-(1/$I$5)*LN(RAND())	=C18-B18	=D18-B18	=D18-C18	=COUNTIF($D$12:D18,">"&B18)	=C18-D17
8	=-(1/$I$4)*LN(RAND())+B18	=IF(D18>B19,D18,B19)	=C19-(1/$I$5)*LN(RAND())	=C19-B19	=D19-B19	=D19-C19	=COUNTIF($D$12:D19,">"&B19)	=C19-D18
9	=-(1/$I$4)*LN(RAND())+B19	=IF(D19>B20,D19,B20)	=C20-(1/$I$5)*LN(RAND())	=C20-B20	=D20-B20	=D20-C20	=COUNTIF($D$12:D20,">"&B20)	=C20-D19
10	=-(1/$I$4)*LN(RAND())+B20	=IF(D20>B21,D20,B21)	=C21-(1/$I$5)*LN(RAND())	=C21-B21	=D21-B21	=D21-C21	=COUNTIF($D$12:D21,">"&B21)	=C21-D20
11	=-(1/$I$4)*LN(RAND())+B21	=IF(D21>B22,D21,B22)	=C22-(1/$I$5)*LN(RAND())	=C22-B22	=D22-B22	=D22-C22	=COUNTIF($D$12:D22,">"&B22)	=C22-D21
12	=-(1/$I$4)*LN(RAND())+B22	=IF(D22>B23,D22,B23)	=C23-(1/$I$5)*LN(RAND())	=C23-B23	=D23-B23	=D23-C23	=COUNTIF($D$12:D23,">"&B23)	=C23-D22
13	=-(1/$I$4)*LN(RAND())+B23	=IF(D23>B24,D23,B24)	=C24-(1/$I$5)*LN(RAND())	=C24-B24	=D24-B24	=D24-C24	=COUNTIF($D$12:D24,">"&B24)	=C24-D23
14	=-(1/$I$4)*LN(RAND())+B24	=IF(D24>B25,D24,B25)	=C25-(1/$I$5)*LN(RAND())	=C25-B25	=D25-B25	=D25-C25	=COUNTIF($D$12:D25,">"&B25)	=C25-D24
15	=-(1/$I$4)*LN(RAND())+B25	=IF(D25>B26,D25,B26)	=C26-(1/$I$5)*LN(RAND())	=C26-B26	=D26-B26	=D26-C26	=COUNTIF($D$12:D26,">"&B26)	=C26-D25

Figure D.1.

Excel Application Information and Tips

Data Analysis Package

The Analysis ToolPak option in Excel needs to be activated for simulations because many of the functions mentioned require it. It is loaded when the software is installed, but for reasons unknown, the user must activate it. Similarly, Excel's Solver option must also be activated by the user. To activate both options, use the appropriate instructions given here.

    Excel Version 2003: Select the Tools menu, scroll down to the Add-Ins choice, select, and you will see a list of add-ins. Click the box for Analysis ToolPak. If not already activated, clicking the boxes for the other choices that do not have VBA (Visual Basic for Applications) at the end would be a good idea for future use in business problems. (VBA is for advanced Excel users who wish to program their own special functions.) Click OK and return to Excel. The data analysis add-in is then found as a choice on the Tools menu.

    Excel Version 2007: Click on the big button in the upper left corner, select Excel Options at the lower right of the menu, then select Add-Ins in the left column of choices. Then check to see if the Analysis ToolPak and the Solver Add-in applications are active. If not, click Go on the Manage Excel Add-ins menu at the bottom and then check the Analysis ToolPak and Solver Add-ins menu that appears and click OK. The Data Analysis and Solver Add-ins are then found on the far right of the Data tab menu.

    Excel Version 2010: The instructions are similar to those for Excel 2007, but you select the File menu to access the Options menu instead of clicking on the big button.

Useful Excel Functions for Simulation Model Creation

Excel has a fairly good help menu for learning new functions. The functions you may find particularly useful for simulations are presented here.

IF Function

Returns one result if the expression is true (e.g., X > 60), another if it is false. By concatenating IF functions, different sets of outcomes can be determined depending on the input conditions.

VLOOKUP and HLOOKUP Functions

These functions are used to select one piece of data in a table based on a correlating piece of data in that table when there is no equation to relate the two values directly. An example would be selecting the arrival rate associated with a given probability of occurrence.

COUNTIF Function

This function (=COUNTIF(range,criteria) is very useful for determining the current line length for a waiting line simulation. Examples are given in the M/M/1 model shown in Figure D.1. The criteria statement in the function to tell it when to count an item is generally easy to set up as illustrated in the Help files, but the criteria here for counting when one cell value in a range of cells is greater than a reference cell value is tricky when that reference cell address keeps changing. That is, the critieria in Figure D.1 is ">" (cell address for customer n's arrival time) and the range is all of the service end times for customers 1 through n − 1.

Descriptive Statistics, Histogram, Regression,
Rank, and Percentile Functions

These functions are found in the Analysis ToolPak. The other functions provided are also useful from time to time, but the descriptive statistics, histogram, regression, rank, and percentile functions are more commonly needed. If you are unfamiliar with using any of these functions, the Excel Help button provided with each function provides a basic tutorial regarding its use:

- Descriptive statistics allows you to select a range of data values and obtain results, such as average, min, max, standard deviation, median, and kurtosis, with just one keystroke.

- Histogram sorts the selected data into bins and can also automatically create a histogram chart of the results. Bin sizes can be specified by you as described in chapter 7, or the function will automatically choose an appropriate bin size if you wish. However, the automatic choice of bin size is likely to reduce the resolution of different arrival rates or service times in discrete probability lookup tables created from the histogram results.
- Regression allows calculating the intercept and slope constants from a set of x and y data in a straight-line approximation of this information.
- Rank and Percentile sorts a set of integer data from highest occurrence to lowest and calculates the percentage for each occurrence value as a percentage of the whole. This function can be useful for determining probabilities for discrete distributions in simulations.

Data Tables

This obscure capability of Excel is useful for summarizing simulation results. For example, when you run a simulation for 100 customers that might represent one day's work and summarize the result—for example, average line length, max and min values—it is laborious to press the F9 key to execute another 100-customer simulation run, repeat the summarization, and so on for perhaps a month's worth of work. Data tables allow you to collect a number of such summaries with one press of the F9 key, a major savings in time for simulation analysis.

The problem is that most Excel handbooks are quite vague about how to set data tables up for simulation runs and even finding the menu for more general use of data tables is difficult. In Excel 2010, the menu is part of the What If Analysis submenu under the Data tab on the toolbar. Chapter 26 in the book by Jelen (2010) has a short discussion of What-If tables (data tables) which is a useful introduction. I attempted to use the Scenario Manager in the Excel 2010 What-IF Analysis menu for setting up a simulation data table, but had no success. The Scenario Manager may be able to help, but at this time I am unable to provide the proper inputs because its nomenclature does not seem to correlate with any familiar simulation terms.

The book by Weida et al. (2001) has a fair introduction to the use of data tables for queuing simulations if you are using an older version of Excel than the 2007 and 2010 versions. Chapter 15 of Winston (2004) provides several examples on how to set them up for one-way and two-way applications. The problem is that to apply them to summarizing simulation data, the handbooks rarely discuss how to use a variable that is not actually used in the calculations (such as the simulation run number) to trigger the number of repetitions desired. Normally, when you use a sequence of run numbers as the one input variable, but do not use it in the data table calculations, all you get is one result. The trick is recognizing that the use of the random number function in the simulation equations causes the results to change each time a run is done. When, and only when, random numbers are involved, you can designate the run numbers as the input variable to trigger the run calculations. Weida et al. (2001) does that in chapter 13.2.2, but it is often tricky to make it work right. The other difficulty is that help searches for data tables often assume that you meant pivot tables, so the search takes you there. But data tables and pivot tables are not the same!

I am working on a much clearer explanation on how to use data tables in later Excel versions for simulation applications, which I plan to include as an appendix in a future revision of this monograph. In the meantime, it might take some effort to get a data table to work for you, but the effort is well worth it.

Notes

Preface

1. Fitzsimmons and Fitzsimmons (2011).

Chapter 1

1. Refer to Appendices A and B for more detailed descriptions of the terms and symbols used in the text.

2. Laguna and Marklund (2005), chapter 6.

3. Hillier and Lieberman (2010), chapter 17.

4. Nelson (2010), chapter 8.

5. Some of you are probably asking, "Shouldn't this value be 50%?" Many of my students ask this question because their familiarity in using normal distributions implies that the average should be at the 50% point. Although this is true for a normal distribution, it is not true for the majority of distributions. For an exponential distribution, the average value corresponds to the 36.78% point and to the $1 - 0.3678 = 63.21\%$ point for the inverse exponential distribution.

6. Abner Krarup Erlang (1878–1929) is a Danish mathematician who developed a number of queuing theory concepts for telephone company applications in the early 1900s. Refer to appendix A for further details.

7. Attributed to the British statistician D. G. Kendall (1918–2007) during the period from 1951 to 1953.

Chapter 2

1. Named after J. D. C. Little, who published a proof of this formula in 1961. The formula had been observed and used by others shortly before Little published his proof.

Chapter 3

1. The single line arrangement is sometimes referred to as a "snake" configuration by some authors because it often requires a winding layout to accommodate

its length. A common example is the arrangement at airports before the passenger security checkpoints.

2. Obviously, a new server is likely to not be as productive as an experienced server. However, keep in mind that the waiting line equations are based on a steady-state condition, which implies that all servers have attained the average service rate capability. How long this may take is discussed in more detail in chapter 5.

3. Note the parentheses added around the summation term in the denominator to clarify that the second term is not to be included in the summation. This addresses a commonly observed mistake by many of my students when we first added waiting line topics to our process and operations management courses.

Chapter 4

1. Pollaczek (1930) and Khintchine (1932). See glossary (appendix A).
2. This use of α should not be confused with its use in Equation (1.2) for the exponential distribution.
3. Peck and Hazelwood (1958).

Chapter 5

1. This is done to simplify the equations for calculating P_0 and L_q because only ρ and the number of servers s is required in these equations. This also agrees with the P_0 and L_q data tables provided for a range of ρ and s values in appendix C. The reader is reminded that ρ here is not the same as $\rho_s = \lambda/\mu s$, the multiple-channel ρ used by some authors.

2. Named after a sixteenth-century French mathematician, L'Hospital or L'Hôpital. When confronted with an expression where it is not possible to define a limit as a variable approaches a certain value (1 in this case), successive derivatives of the numerator and the denominator with respect to that variable are taken until they converge to a definable limit.

3. The term "finite queuing table" is not exactly correct for this situation since we are discussing finite sources here, not finite queues. The term is more appropriate for our earlier discussion regarding limited line capacity. However, this term is used in many textbooks for both capacity and sourcing issues because it is consistent with its usage by Peck and Hazelwood (1958), a commonly used resource for solving finite sourcing problems.

4. Krajewski et al. (2010).

Chapter 6

1. Bekker (2005) is a good overall reference; Hillier and Lieberman (2010) discuss this in chapter 17, section 17.5.

2. If you are unfamiliar with service blueprints, the article by Shostack (1984) is a good introduction.

3. One utility cost often forgotten is waste management. A good waste management policy can help keep this cost low and reduce the number of staff required to support it.

4. This material was formerly chapter 18 in the previous edition of this reference.

5. McCarran Airport in Las Vegas does this in an effective and entertaining way by showing video clips on conveniently placed video monitors in the security check-in process area. The clips are of local Las Vegas Strip entertainers doing or being corrected for not doing the right thing at different check-in steps.

6. Some Disney theme parks let customers buy tickets for popular rides, where the ticketing system calculates the average waiting time until the ticket holder can board the next available ride and prints that time on the ticket. This allows customers to visit other parts of the park, such as food and retail shops, instead of waiting in line. Longer waits are then not as significant, and park visitors can even go and buy other tickets for rides later in the day. The ticketing system's job in forecasting the average waiting time is simplified because the service time (the duration of the ride) is essentially constant. The somewhat hidden advantage here is that park revenue from food and retail shops is less affected by lost customer visits while they wait in line at the rides.

7. Abilla (2007).

8. This constrains us to a fixed appointment time during the day because we cannot predict when these urgent-care situations will occur during the day. For doctors who are not expected to handle such drop-in patients, we have more flexibility regarding the length of the appointment times, allowing a mixture of short appointments and long appointments according to patient needs. Then we can even use short-term scheduling rules to schedule the order in which patients are offered appointment times.

9. These values used here should not be construed to represent all medical practices. When a full range of medical services is being provided and urgent care patients must be accommodated, these values are typically larger and have greater variance.

10. As a note of interest, the need to accommodate some urgent-care patients is often greater at the beginning and ending of the week. This is likely caused by the more limited availability of health care professionals on weekends.

11. For those interested in learning more about reservation systems and overbooking, chapter 11 in Fitzsimmons and Fitzsimmons (2011) is a good introduction.

12. Hillier and Lieberman (2010), chapter 17.

13. Haussmann (1970).

14. It should be noted that the benefits of dequeuing can also be achieved by educating the customers waiting in line as to what will be required when they

reach the server window, allowing them to fill out such forms in advance while they are waiting. This gives them something to do while also improving line performance.

15. Stevenson (2011), chapter 16.

16. Jacobs and Chase (2011), chapter 19.

17. While we do not show a specific example of how makespan can be used for waiting line management, one example would be estimating how long it would usually take to process customers remaining to be served after normal closing time.

Chapter 7

1. Little (1961).

2. If you are unfamiliar with how to create histograms in Excel using the function provided in Excel's Analysis ToolPak, refer to the Excel tips section in appendix D.

3. Where this value comes from was commented on earlier for the discussion regarding exponential distributions in chapter 1.

Appendix A

1. Named for D. R. Cox (1995).

2. Named for the Danish mathematician Agner Krarup Erlang (1878–1929). His work with the Copenhagen Telephone Company in the early 1900s provided the foundation for several aspects of modern waiting line analysis.

3. Kendall (1951). This method is commonly indicated by the generic A/B/C/d/e/f notation. The last three characteristics are not shown in many textbooks; those that do use them often do not follow the order given in the definition above.

4. Named for the Russian mathematician Andrey Andreyevich Markov (1856–1922). Sometimes the term *Markovian process* is restricted to describing sequences of independent random variables with continuous values, such as those defined by exponential distributions. When this is done, similar sequences of discrete variables are referred to as Markov chains.

5. Named for Felix Pollaczek and Aleksandr Khintchine. Each independently developed this formula, in 1930 and 1932, respectively. Many citations of their formula have a wide range of spelling variations for Khintchine.

Appendix D

1. See Fitzsimmons & Fitzsimmons (2011), p. 438, for the reasoning behind the derivation of this expression. For a more convenient method than using 12 random numbers for each value required, use Excel's NORM.INV function.

References

You can find many useful queuing analysis references on the Internet, but many search listings containing the term *queuing* are likely to refer to communication network or software programming applications. Some useful references are listed here; using their titles in search engines as starting points are more likely to lead to the types of articles you are looking for.

Abilla, P. (2007). *Psychology of queuing & Disneyland* [Web log post]. Retrieved July 28, 2011 from http://www.shmula.com/psychology-of-queueing-disneyland/372

Bekker, R. (2005). *Queues with state-dependent rates.* Eindhoven, The Netherlands: Technische Universiteit Eindhoven. Retrieved July 30, 2011 from http://alexandria.tue.nl/extra2/200513578.pdf

Bozarth, C. C., & Handfield, R. B. (2008). *Introduction to operations and supply chain management* (2nd ed.). Upper Saddle River, NJ: Prentice Hall.

Chander, H. (2006). *Contracts in outsourcing.* Retrieved March 10, 2011, from http://www.math.vu.nl/en/Images/werkstuk-chander_tcm72-94371.doc

Easton, F. F. (2002). *Labor requirements for multi-server multi-class finite queues.* Retrieved March 10, 2011, from http://myweb.whitman.syr.edu/ffeaston/Research/Mmck_2cl.PDF

Fitzsimmons, J. A., & Fitzsimmons, M. J. (2011). *Service management: Operations, strategy, information technology* (7th ed.). New York, NY: McGraw-Hill.

Grasing, R. E. (2011). *Branch performance by the new numbers.* Retrieved July 24, 2011 from http://www.renolan.com/banking/article-branch_performance_by_the_new_numbers.htm

Haussmann, R. K. D. (1970). Waiting time as an index of quality of nursing care. *Health Services Research, Summer,* 92–105. Retrieved July 29, 2011, from http://www.ncbi.nlm.nih.gov/pmc/articles/PMC1067272/pdf/hsresearch00575-0014.pdf

Heizer, J., & Render, B. (2008). *Operations management* (9th ed.). Upper Saddle River, NJ: Prentice Hall.

Heyde, C. C., & Seneta, E. (Eds.). (2001). *Statisticians of the centuries.* New York, NY: Springer-Verlag.

Hillier, F. S., & Lieberman, G. J. (2010). *Introduction to operations research* (9th ed.). New York, NY: McGraw-Hill.

Jacobs, F. R., & Chase, R. B. (2011). *Operations and supply chain management* (13th ed.). New York, NY: McGraw-Hill.

Jardine, A. K. S., & Tsang, A. H. C. (2005). *Maintenance, replacement, and reliability: Theory and applications.* Boca Raton, FL: CRC Press.

Jelen, B. (2010). *Microsoft 2010 Excel in depth.* Indianapolis, IN: Que.

Khintchine, A. Y. (1932). Mathematical theory of a stationary queue. *Matematicheskii Sbornik* 39(4): 73–84.

Koenigsberg, E. (1960). Finite queues and cyclic queues. *Operations Research,* 8(2), 246–253.

Koerts, J. (1963). On mean waiting times and their reduction by priority procedures: An expository survey and some tables. *Statistica Neerlandica, 17*(3), 267–283. Retrieved from http://onlinelibrary.wiley.com/doi/10.1111/j.1467-9574.1963.tb01045.x/abstract

Kotha, S. K., Barnum, M. P., & Bowen, D. A. (1996). KeyCorp Service Excellence Management System. *Interfaces* 26(1), 54–74.

Krajewski, L. J., Ritzman, L. P., & Malhotra, M. K. (2010). *Operations management: Processes and supply chains* (9th ed.). Upper Saddle River, NJ: Prentice Hall.

Laguna, M., & Marklund, J. (2005). *Business process modeling, simulation, and design.* Upper Saddle River, NJ: Prentice-Hall.

Little, J. D. C. (1961). A proof of the queuing formula: $L = \lambda W$. *Operations Research, 9*(3), 383–387.

Maister, D. H. (1985). *The psychology of waiting lines.* Retrieved July 28, 2011 from http://davidmaister.com/articles/5/52

Nelson, B. L. (2010). *Stochastic modeling: Analysis & simulation.* Mineola, NY: Dover.

Norman, D. A. (2008). *The psychology of waiting lines.* Retrieved July 28, 2011 from http://www.jnd.org/ms/Norman%20The%20Psychology%20of%20Waiting%20Lines.pdf

Oldrich, V. (1967). *On the preemptive priority queues.* Retrieved July 29, 2011, from http://www.kybernetika.cz/content/1967/2/147/paper.pdf

Peck, L. G., & Hazelwood, R. N. (1958). Finite queuing tables. In *Publications in Operations Research* (Vol. 2). New York, NY: John Wiley & Sons.

Pollaczek, F. (1930). Über eine aufgabe der wahrscheinlichkeitstheorie. *Mathematische Zeitschrift* 32: 64–100.

Shostack, G. L. (1984). Designing services that deliver. *Harvard Business Review,* 84115: 133–139. Retrieved July 27, 2011, from http://www.semanticfoundry.com/docs/servicesThatDeliver.pdf

Stevenson, W. J. (2011). *Operations management* (11th ed.). New York, NY: McGraw-Hill.

Sztrik, J. (2001). *Finite-source queuing systems and their applications: A bibliography.* Retrieved March 10, 2011, from http://irh.inf.unideb.hu/user/jsztrik/research/fsqreview.pdf

Vignaux, G. A. (2007). *The bank: An example of a SimPy simulation.* Retrieved March 10, 2011 from http://simpy.sourceforge.net/SimPyDocs/TheBank.html

Weida, N. C., Richardson, R., & Vazsonyi, A. (2001). *Operations analysis using Microsoft Excel.* Pacific Grove, CA: Duxbury–Thomson Learning.

Winston, W. L. (2004). *Microsoft Excel data analysis and business modeling.* Redmond, WA: Microsoft Press.

Index

A

alternate arrival time distributions, 43–45

alternate service time distributions, 38–43

appointment schedule analysis, 96–97

arrival, 127
   distribution, 127

arrival rate, 127
   management methods, 94–99

B

back office, 127

balance equations, 11–13, 127

balking, 127

birth and death process, 128

blocking, 128

C

calling population, 7, 128

Central Limit Theorem, 40, 128

channel, 128

coefficient of variation, 128

coffee shops
   different service distributions, 42
   with limited capacity, 47
   with one server, 21–22
   with two servers, 31–32

continuous distribution determination, 108–111

cost curves, 15–16

coxian distribution, 128

customers
   classes, 65
   priorities, 65–66

D

data analysis package, 151

data tables, 153–154

dequeue, 128

deterministic, 128–129

discrete distribution determination, 111–115

discrete probability distributions, 108–115

E

earliest due date (EDD), 101

Erlang delay system, 59

Erlang distribution, 10, 129

Erlang loss function, 129

Erlang loss system, 59

Excel applications, 151–154

exponential distribution, 9–10

F

factory inventory costs, 83

first come, first served (FCFS) priority rule, 14, 129

first in, first out (FIFO) priority rule, 14, 101, 129

front office, 129

G

Grasing, R. E., 68–69

H

Hazelwood, R. N., 54, 63

helicopter shuttle business costs, 82

Hillier, F. S., 7, 54, 79, 82, 101

I

ice cream shop with limited customer space, 83

improving service performance, 83–91

interarrival distribution, 129

interarrival time, 129

inverse probability distributions, 149

J
jockeying, 129
Johnson's Rule, 101

K
Kendall notation, 13, 17, 27, 43, 45, 48, 129
Kotha, S. K., 68

L
Laguna, M., 7, 54, 125
learning curves, 67
Lieberman, G. J., 7, 54, 79, 82, 101
limited calling population, 48–54, 61–65
limited capacity, 45–48, 59–61
line configurations, 66
line length, 130
Little's Law, 3, 19, 103–104, 130

M
makespan, 130
managerial considerations, 71–102
Marklund, J., 7, 54, 125
Markovian process, 130
memoryless, 130
multiple-channel
    application data, 139–148
    models, 57–69
    single-phase model, 25–35
multiple phases, 54–55

N
Nelson, B. L., 7
nonpreemptive priorities, 100–102
notation, 13–14

O
overbooking, 99

P
PASTA, 130
Peck, L. G., 54, 63
performance measures, 5–7
phase, 130
phase-type distribution, 130
point of sale (POS), 131
Poisson distribution, 8–9

Pollaczek-Khintchine (P-K) formula, 38, 130–31
preemptive priorities, 100–102
priority management, 99–102
priority queue, 131
priority rules, 14–15, 131
probability of zero customers, 131
psychological factors, waiting line configurations, 91–94

Q
queue, 131

R
random number approximations of probability distributions, 121–125
reneging, 131
repair service
    with multiple servers, 63–65
    with one server, 50–53

S
sandwich stand cost trade-offs, 79–82
service
    blueprint, 131
    capability variations, 66–69
    distribution, 131
    rate, 132
    time, 132
    time reduction learning rates, 68–69
shortest process time first (SPT), 101
simulation information, 149–154
simulation models, 116–120, 151–152
single-channel, single-phase model, 17–24
sojourn time, 132
state-dependent rate, 132
state-dependent variance, 72
state diagrams, 11–13, 132
stochastic, 132
symbols defined, 135–137
system, 20

U
utilization factor, 132–133

V
variance and risk considerations, 72–74
variation reduction, 84

W
waiting line
   configurations, psychological fac-
      tors, 91–94

costs, 74–83, 133
data collection, 104–108
models, 13–14
theory, 1
waiting time, 133
Weida, N. C., 125, 154
Winston, W. L., 125, 154
work in process (WIP), 133

Announcing the Business Expert Press Digital Library

Concise E-books Business Students
Need for Classroom and Research

This book can also be purchased in an e-book collection by your library as

- a one-time purchase,
- that is owned forever,
- allows for simultaneous readers,
- has no restrictions on printing,
- can be downloaded as PDFs from within the library community.

Our digital library collections are a great solution to beat the rising cost of textbooks. E-books can be loaded into their course management systems or onto students' e-book readers.

The **Business Expert Press** digital libraries are very affordable, with no obligation to buy in future years.

For more information, please visit **www.businessexpertpress.com/librarians**. To set up a trial in the United States, please contact **Sheri Dean** at sheri.dean@globalepress.com; for all other regions, contact **Nicole Lee** at nicole.lee@igroupnet.com.

OTHER TITLES IN OUR QUANTITATIVE APPROACHES TO DECISION MAKING COLLECTION

- *Working With Sample Data: Exploration and Inference* by Priscilla Chaffe-Stengel and Donald N. Stengel
- *Working With Time Series Data: Analysis and Forecasting* by Donald N. Stengel and Priscilla Chaffe-Stengel
- *Business Applications of Multiple Regression* by Ronny Richardson

CPSIA information can be obtained at www.ICGtesting.com
Printed in the USA
BVOW020619231211

278971BV00006B/1/P